WOMEN'S REBELLION & ISLAMIC MEMORY

About the author

Fatima Mernissi, perhaps the most famous feminist scholar of the Middle East, was born in 1940 in Fez, Morocco. She studied political science and sociology at Mohammad V University, where she subsequently taught from 1974 to 1980. She has published prolifically in both French and Arabic. Previous translations of her work into English include *Beyond the Veil* (Indiana University Press/Al Saqi); *Doing Daily Battle* (Women's Press/Rutgers University Press); *The Veil and the Male Elite* (Addison Wesley), published in the UK as *Women and Islam* (Blackwell); *The Forgotten Queens of Islam* (Polity Press/University of Minnesota Press); *Islam and Democracy* (Addison Wesley/Virago); and *Dreams of Trespass* (Addison Wesley), published in the UK as *The Harem Within* (Doubleday).

FATIMA MERNISSI

WOMEN'S
REBELLION
&
ISLAMIC
MEMORY

ZED BOOKS
London & New Jersey

Women's Rebellion and Islamic Memory was first published by
Zed Books Ltd, 7 Cynthia Street, London N1 9JF, UK,
and 165 First Avenue, Atlantic Highlands,
New Jersey 07716, USA
in 1996.

Cover design by Andrew Corbett.
Typeset by Photosetting and Secretarial Services Ltd, Yeovil
Printed and bound in the United Kingdom by
Biddles Ltd, Guildford and Kings Lynn

A catalogue record for this book is available from the British Library.

US CIP is available from the Library of Congress.

ISBN 1 85649 397 0 Hb
ISBN 1 85649 398 9 Pb

Contents

Introduction   vii

I   **Writing is Better than a Face-lift**   1

II   **Rebuild Baghdad? But in What Galaxy?**   8

III   **Morocco: The Merchant's Daughter and the
            Son of the Sultan**   13

            The Merchant's Daughter and the Son of the Sultan / 16

IV   **Women, Saints and Sanctuaries**   21

            Sanctuaries as Therapy / 23 Sanctuaries as Anti-
            establishment Arenas / 25   Sainthood as an Alternative
            to Male-defined Femininity / 27   Male Saints as Anti-
            heroes / 29

V   **Virginity and Patriarchy**   34

            The Link between Women and Nature / 34 The Lack of
            Understanding between the Sexes / 35 The Great
            Tragedy of the Patriarchal Male / 37 Social
            Schizophrenia / 38 The Consequences of Inequality / 40
            Social Changes and the Reorganization of Space / 41 The
            Pursuit of Adolescent Girls / 43 The Symptom of
            Malaise / 44

VI   **Population Planning Without Democracy?
            The Conflict between the Muslim State
            and Women**   46

            I The Unbridled Sexuality of Women as the Cause of the
            Population Explosion / 46
            II The Notion of Ante-natal Care as a Revolution in the
            Relations between Women and the Muslim State: Female
            reproduction and male administative efficiency / 49
            III Why is the Ineffectiveness of the Public Services in
            Women's Issues not Perceived as a Scandal? The notions
            of *qaid* and *hijab* as obstacles to citizenship / 55
            IV Women's Education and their Participation in the
            Process of Democratization, particularly in Media

Production, as Two Ways of Promoting the Wider Use of
Birth Control / 58 Conclusion / 60

VII   **Women's Work**   63

Religious and Scientific Concepts as Political
Manipulation in Dependent Islam / 63 Sex Roles in
Medieval Islam / 68 The *Jariya*: History and Legend / 69

VIII   **The *Jariya* and the Caliph:**
Thoughts on the Place of Women in Muslim
Political Memory   77

Pertinence of the Problematic and Definition of Concepts
/ 77 Problematic / 79 Conclusion: What is to be Done
with an Anti-democratic 'Political Memory'? / 89

IX   **Women in Muslim History:**
Traditional Perspectives and New Strategies   92

Medieval History and the Legitimization of Women's Rights
/ 95 Stategies for Enhancing the Image of Muslim
Women / 100

X   **Femininity as Subversion: Reflection on the**
Muslim Concept of *Nushuz*   109

Individualism as a Crime Against the Sacred Law: The
Concept of *Bid'a* and Its Proximity to the Concept of
Nushuz / 111 Sakina and A'isha: Feminists of the First
Century of Islam / 113 Sakina's Rebellion: The First
Century / 114 Feminism as an Internal Threat to Muslim
Order: Implications of *Nushuz* / 115 Conclusion: The
Umma and the Challenge of Individualism(s) / 118

Index   121

Introduction

In this bleak, crisis-ridden, post-Gulf War period, we must ask whether there are any links, any connections, between two seemingly unrelated phenomena: (1) the veiling of women acclaimed by the oil emirs and shaykhs in the 1980s as an ideal, and sometimes enforced as a state religious programme, and (2) the growth of terrorism justified on religious grounds that is appearing in many of our Muslim capitals. What does the veiling of women, claimed as a sacred ideal, and enforced in many oil-rich countries such as Saudi Arabia as a state policy, have to do with this wave of religion-based terrorism? I want to suggest in this short introduction that, with civilians dying daily in the blooded streets of Cairo and Algiers in the deadlock between state and fundamentalist opposition, both the veil campaigns of the 1980s and terrorism of the 1990s have to do with the barbarous silencing of citizens and, the deliberate strategies to block democratic process. The waves of religion based on terrorism in the 1990s are the tormented response of a mutilated Muslim society whose progressive forces have been savagely emasculated, and the systematic campaigns to veil half the population were some of the effective means used to achieve that emasculation. This book attempts to understand from different angles the puzzling question that is my obsession: why on earth is the Arab world so hostile to women? Why can it not see women as a key force for development building? Why so much desire to humiliate and retard us, despite our efforts to educate ourselves and become productive and useful? Why have we been the target of constant rejections and exclusions? I tried to find the answer in history ('Women in Muslim History', 'Feminism as Subversion' and later 'La Jarya et le Khalife'), in economics ('Women's Work'), religion ('Women, Saints and Sanctuaries') and finally demography. But it was only with the Gulf War that the mystery of this hostility towards women became clear: it was not so much a war against femininity that was going on, as a war against democracy. Women happened to be an easy group to manipulate because they were unorganized and therefore powerless, but also because of a rich tradition of misogyny which was heavily revived and technologically backed (television, state monopoly over school textbooks etc.). The Gulf War showed the obscenity of the Arab state: its function was not to defend the interests of the citizen, it was to crush any chance of building a civil society and to censure any attempts to check on what the chiefs were doing. The Gulf War showed, for example, that although the military expenditures in our Arab world were the highest in the world, since our states bought 40 per cent of the arms sold in the world in the 1980s, they were grotesque in their uselessness during the Gulf conflict. 'The Middle East remains the world's principal market for arms and military equipment. In 1987, the region as a whole imported some 17.9 billion in arms, almost 38 per scent of the world's principal market for arms and military equipment. ['In 1897, the region as a whole imported some 17.9 billion in arms, almost 38per cent of the world market'.]

In fact this surrealist investment in useless arms purchases by states where demographic explosion was alarming, and where youth unemployment was soaring, would not have been possible if progressive forces had been encouraged to play their role as the builders of civil society. Such a decision to divert resources towards sterile arms imports would not have been possible had government officials and cabinet ministers been accountable and their policies debated and checked by citizens. Moreover, the Gulf War exposed the role of petrodollar-engineered Islam and the investment of the oil countries, with Saudi Arabia in the lead, in the strengthening of conservative, extreme right-wing movements, as a way of weakening civil society, and why for such a state the veiling of women was so strategic. 'Rebuild Baghdad' and 'Writing is Better than a Face-lift', written after the war, give an idea of how it felt to be an Arab woman and to come to realize, after decades of analysis, that the state officials, bureaucrats and apparatchiks, who crushed our hopes and chances of achieving some dignity and of enjoying our rights and becoming responsible citizens capable of debating issues and designing alternatives, were in fact mediocre nonentities who had no power but that of the swords they held over our heads. Not only did the bureaucrats of the Arab states squander our resources, but they made women their strategic target in paralysing civil liberties.

Campaigns ordering women to veil in the 1980s had multiple, almost magical, multi-sequential effects. The first was that the veil worked as powerful counter-democracy offensive, since the female half of the population was ordered to make itself invisible, and instructed to step back into the domestic sphere and refrain from interfering in the public sphere. If women were to be reminded that they have no business in the public sphere, it was clear that the other half of the population was not going to be granted such privilege. Second was that the veil issue diverted attention, quite successfully, from the pressing soaring unemployment problem, due mainly to uncontrolled demographic explosion. The Arab population increased by 29 million between 1985 and 1990. With one of the highest birth rates in the world (3.9per cent), the Arab world population, estimated to be 188 millions in 1985, reached 217 million in 1990. But instead of Arab states forcing their citizens to debate the key issue of an unplanned population explosion, which was likely to jeopardize all kinds of social and economic policies—such as in the spheres of education and health—and employment opportunities, and individual responsibility of both men and women by strengthening progressive forces, fortifying parties, trade unions and non-governmental associations, the opposite was planned. Not only were progressive forces crushed by classical authoritarian means such as harassment and imprisonment of intellectuals, the banning of books and stifling of dissent through the banning of associations, but huge oil resources were invested in fabricating an anti-democratic culture by the promotion of a petro-Islam propagated by interior ministries, whose main message was blind obedience to the chief.

At the beginning of the 1970s the systematic funding of religious conservative movements was launched as a pan-Arab state programme, with President Sadat as one of its key engineers. 'Anwar Sadat had come to power and had already begun to reverse many of Nasser's policies. Nasserites and Communists were officially branded as enemies of the regime. Since Sadat had no power base of his own other than the Army, the decision was made to cultivate the political right—particularly the religious right. Thus, in 1971, with Sadat's encouragement, King Faisal of Saudi Arabia—in what amounted to a unique treaty between a state and a foreign religious institution—offered Sheikh Abdel Halim Mahmoud, the rector of Al-Azhar (the famous religious University of Cairo and the main centre of Islamic learning), $100 million to conduct a campaign against communism and atheism, and for the triumph of Islam.... There was a lavish publicity campaign: books were written, new mosques were built, students were recruited.'

Petro-funded Islam had as a goal the stifling of democratic debate in the Arab world. Birth control and the subsequent unemployment and migration of youth were cruelly ignored, leading to the situation we are now in, with thousands of young people trying to leave their wretched authoritarian countries as clandestine migrants to Europe, and others leaping into militant Islamic protest, sometimes slipping into violent terrorist extremism. When European countries then erect their frontiers like a harem citadel, this does not help solve the migration problem, and we thus have the horror scenes described by a Spanish economist,

Graciela Malgesini: 'Nearly every day off the Mediterranean coast of Spain, wealthy windsurfers unfold their multicoloured sails and plunge into the waters. As often as the wind invites acrobatic risk-taking on the crests of the waves, it turns the straits into a graveyard for hundreds of Moroccan migrants. More than 200 drowned between January and October 1992 alone. Their journeys occur under conditions of extraordinary risk and with minimal chance of success. Many are captured the moment they set foot on Spanish soil, or even while still at sea. During the first ten months of 1992, 2,000 undocumented immigrants were detained on the shores of Cadiz; in 1991, 2,500 were captured in Andalusia alone. This risk they evidently prefer to the desperate poverty that motivated their flight.' When asked why they decided to migrate, many of the youth answered: 'Death is better than misery.' To understand the sweeping waves of extremism and the fanatical protest movements in today's Mediterranean area, one has to keep in mind the other, non-televised scene–that of desperate young people of both sexes (who have no way of affecting decision-making), who jump into unsafe boats going to a fantasy Europe that no longer exists. Clandestine migration and fanatic militarism have to be traced to where they belong: the choking of civil society by national and international interest groups and lobbies. The Gulf is a gigantic illustration of that scenario.

Instead of alerting public opinion to the population explosion and trying to analyse its causes, which would have led to the identification of women's illiteracy and consequent economic marginalization as factors, Arab states were busy promoting the veil, despite the fact that international population studies have shown the education of women to be one of the means to curb the birth rate. And since there has been no serious state comprehensive and democracy-based approach to the population problem, which would have meant promoting women, it is expected that by the year 2000, 64 Arab babies are expected to be born every day. The Arab population would by then have reached 281 million. This means, if one remembers that roughly two thirds of the population are under 25 years of age, that the number of jobs to be created to face the year 2000 demographic explosion is estimated to be 145 million. If rich and developed nations of the European economic market are admitting to recession, and their governments have to come up every day with explanations to their citizens about how they intend to create the few million jobs they need to reach full employment, Arab governments do not have to explain anything at all. They are busy avoiding any discussion about bleak economic problems, all they want is to divert the discussion from religion, and to moralize about financial, fiscal and commerical issues. The sexual behaviour of the woman, what she does with her body, how she combs and covers her hair are enforced through state-controlled television, as survival issues on which depends the future of nations. And that is indeed an important function of the veil in history of the modern Arab state.

The veil, 'Hijab' in Arabic, means 'curtain'. It has to do with preventing transparency, with putting something out of sight. It goes without saying that I am not talking about a woman deciding for herself, without any pressure from a politician or a husband, to put a scarf on her head and cover her hair and face. That veil is a free initiative and pertains to cosmetic choice and personal hair or facial grooming. The veil I am referring to in this introduction is an intrinsically political one, it is that head-covering forced on women by political authority such as Imam Khomeini's July 1980 'Hijab law' which ordered women working in the state sector to veil, or the Saudi police-enforced veil. Women are not allowed to walk with hair uncovered in Saudi streets; even foreign women are forced to conform to the head-covering order. Yes, veil and terrorism have much in common when you think about it; both breed and thrive in spaces where self-expression is cruelly censored, and where the politicians have opted deliberately and in cold blood to check the democratic process as a way to ensure their survival. The veiling of women as a political ideal and terrorism are but strange, dream-like sex-distorted mirror images of the same fierce garroting of citizens' voices and the pitiless choking of their desire to self-expression. They are mirror images of the same mutilation of self-expression, but while the veil concerns women, terrorism is primarily a man's affair. The enforcement of the veil as state religion-justified policy by Muslim oil leaders as different in their backgrounds as Imam Khomeini and the King of Saudi Arabia in the 1980s was not so much a sex-targeted, religion-inspired , spirituality-inclined endeavour, as many believed it to be. The 1980s' oil-rich statesman's incredibly aggressive veil obsession was not in fact an offensive targeted at women, it was an assault on democratic process, and an attack on civil society's burgeoning hopes. The high priority was to avoid transparency at the level of political decision-making, and veiling 50 per cent of the population, that is women, was at the same time the medium and the message as Macluhan would say; i.e. shut up and stay invisible. And the message was for both sexes, although only one was used as a passive actor in the political theatre scene.

Why are there so many Muslim male politicians, I kept asking myself throughout the 1980s, screaming at us women in the name of 'their understanding' of religion and sacred tradition to throw veils over our

hair, hide our bosoms in heavy chadors, and make us walk modestly with
our eyes to the floor in trembling silence? Could they not, I wondered,
if their aim is to bring us to Islam (in case we go astray, which is their
theory), have stumbled on the beautiful Islam of the Prophet
Mohammed that emerged in my research into the first decade of the
Muslim calendar (622–632 of the Christian calendar) in Medina, and
became the substance of my book *Women and Islam*, as a defender of
women's dignity and opened the mosques to women on an equal footing
with men? Why do these politicians-turned-Imams come up with an anti-
dignity reading of Islam focussed on obedience? How come they do not
see all the incredible wealth of woman-enhancing historical data they
could draw on to build a human rights-nurtured Islam? In the article,
'Women in Muslim History', which was the seed and the beginning of
the reflection culminating in *Women and Islam*, one gets a sense of how
easy it would be to find data from the religious scriptures and classical
history to sustain human rights and women's dignity–if that were the
goal of the Muslim states and the political leadership, and the contesting
groups who claim religion as a base. But evidently, that was not what
the oil-rich Imams and Emirs were looking for. They turned to the past
and to our most cherished spiritual tradition, Islam as creed and history
and rich collective memory, to look for executioners and strengthen their
authority to censure and aggress.

Petro-Islam was financed to mask the obvious: the squandering of
both energy and human resources, so that the chiefs could keep on
exercising their authoritarian power unchecked. And checking on what
the politicians were doing was indeed what Muslims in general, and
women in particular, needed to do badly in the 1980s. If women had
the right to check on what state planners were doing, their real problems,
which were beyond hair-dos and face covers, would have been
addressed. Chief among them would have been illiteracy, a just minimum
wage and social security, and indeed birth control. Women's illiteracy in
many Muslim states is staggering, and is among the highest in the world.
More than 80 per cent of women are illiterate in Mauritania, Sudan and
Somalia, according to a Unesco study on the Arab world. Illiteracy
among women in Saudi Arabia reaches 75 per cent, two thirds of women
in Morocco are illiterate, as is half of the female population of Algeria,
Libya, Tunisia and Egypt, according to the same Unesco source. But
that never seemed to be a national emergency issue for politicians who
claimed that Islam was their concern, forgetting that one outstanding
ethical feature of this religion is solidarity within the group, the sharing
of resources and opportunities. A genuinely concerned Muslim head of
state could not have overlooked illiteracy, this incredible mutilation

experienced by many women as blindness in a world where decoding information, reading and writing have become basic human rights.

If these states had developed comprehensive global strategies to fight female illiteracy in the eighties, instead of financing orders of obedience marketed as religious tradition, the problem of demographic pressure would also have been solved. Statistical analyses in the Third World have shown since the beginning of the 1980s that the best birth control is the education of women. Statistical surveys show that an illiterate Moroccan woman is likely to give birth to five or six children. If she gets access to primary education, she is likely to have only four children. Secondary education brings the woman to think in terms of life quality for both herself and her children, and she starts devising plans to secure a more balanced matching of her resources, and reduces her pregnancies. Extreme poverty, of which illiteracy is a strong indicator, does not allow a woman to see herself as an autonomous agent, able to control and direct her life. The solution to demographic pressure and to the now highly problematic migration in the Mediterranean area does indeed lie with women. But as I have sketched in 'Planification des Naissances', the solution is not to force women to consume pills, it is to give them a chance to participate in building their own economic and political autonomy. And that brings us again to the famous, obsessive question: Why so much hostility towards us women?—a question that keeps popping up whenever I think about our absurd surrealist Arab world, where we have more than enough energy resources and human talents to emerge as a balanced, harmoniously managed, ethically aware world power, but where mismanagement, sorrow and violence are our pitiful daily bread.

Why can't politicians look at our hair and appreciate a Muslim woman standing defiant, her shoulders back, her breast advanced, her eyes boldly scrutinizing them? Why don't our politicians appreciate our hairdos, our bare faces and our direct looks. For many years I wondered why our modest demeanour and self-effacing, accepting, victim-like silent bowing of the head is their sole obssession? Why do they all dream of this fully veiled, self-deprecating creature? What is the mystery of this political dream that permeates all Muslim political arenas, from right to left, from officially established regimes to clandestine oppositions? Why are Muslim men who enter the realm of politics, whether as Emir when they can control the oil, or as president of the republic when there is no oil in sight, suddenly seized by the obsessive dream of the self-effacing, mechanically bowing, eternally silent lady?

Some summer afternoons, weary of it all, sitting on my balcony overlooking Temara beach, some 10km from Rabat, watching the thousands of young men and women in t-shirts, jeans and sneakers, who walk miles from the small ill-equipped, single rooms and unlit streets of their shanty towns to reach the beaches of the Atlantic Ocean, I wonder how long this Arab world, on the verge of stumbling into the 21st century, can afford the non-dialogue between state and youth in general, state and women in particular. I wonder how long the Arab politicians will keep alive the dream of the obedient woman, while the women themselves have deserted not only the traditional roles, but also the traditional male fantasies, to create new ones—like walking miles to the beach to swim. Would it not be better to establish special schools to create the traditional women our politicians desire, and leave us to run things and organize our enormous resources democratically and intelligently?

Maybe we should. Maybe we should think about creating schools to brainwash our politicians out of their obsessive desire for obedient, head-bowed, subservient, silent women. Maybe Muslim women should think about a 'Liberation Vaccine' with which to inoculate our Muslim leaders; from the moment we see a child interested in politics we should give him the chemical he needs in order for him to accept an autonomous self-reliant woman. We certainly need to help these men face reality, to see that the obedient creature has disappeared from earth—and the earth includes the Arab world! No 'cultural specificity' can save Muslim politicians from having to face independent women, in the same way as our 'sacred culture' was unable to prevent the banning by the British and French colonial powers in 1807 of the slavery fought for by the Arab states. The Arab ruling classes defended slavery and resisted its banning for almost a century, until the act of buying and selling slaves was criminalized and punished. Until the year 1956, a Saudi delegate to the United Nations declared that between 150,000 and 500,000 were living as slaves in his country. But for God's sake, we women are not going to wait until the year 2000 for our leaders to relinquish their fantasy of the subservient woman-pet.

Last summer, pondering all this, I could only find a slogan. Instead of: 'Put a Tiger in your Tank!', I thought of 'Put a Powerful Woman in your Brain!' —as part of a publicity campaign financed by Muslim women and directed at our leaders. What would be wonderful—and the start of a cultural revolution—would be to pay for it with petrodollars.

So—Good Reading! And don't forget, unless we find a way to change the Emirs' fantasy, we are not going to change Wall Street. Because, you see, the Emirs need Wall Street and Wall Street needs the Emirs. And neither the Muslim nor the Heretic Capitalist lands have the need for independent, self-reliant women.

Does anyone know how we can get out of this labyrinth? Maybe by reading the chapters in this book—desperate attempts to understand what was going on in my life and the lives of millions like me—you can find alternatives to the vaccine, the publicity, and the brainwashing school for Emirs.

Fatima Mernissi

CHAPTER I

Writing is Better than a Face-lift

Apply *Writing* every day. Your skin will be revitalized by its wonderful properties! From the moment you wake, *Writing* promotes cellular activity. With the very first marks on the blank page, those bags under your eyes fade right away and your skin feels fresh again. By noon, it is in tip-top condition. With its active ingredients, *Writing* reinforces your epidermic structure. At the end of the day, your wrinkles have faded and your features are smooth again.

Just try writing for a few days. In the end, it's every bit as effective as *Résistance*, the skin cream whose advertising copy I've borrowed here. What have you to lose? Nothing. And in fact you save on the cost of the cream. Writing costs you just the price of a biro (1 dirham-DH)[1], an exercise book (1.50DH) and the odd few stolen hours, strung together like pearls on a necklace.

Start tomorrow. Put your moisturizing cream away, get up an hour earlier and sit yourself down with a pen in front of a blank page. And bring some patience to the task. Lots of patience. Suddenly, things will happen. The page will come alive, your brain will click into gear, your body will be energized and your ideas will come together.

Writing, I tell you, is the best remedy for all kinds of crises, all types of wrinkles. The only thing it really can't cure is greying hair. You'll have to use henna for that. But, in spite of my nationalistic attachment to tradition, I have to admit that henna is uncontrollable. At times my hair comes out carrot-coloured, at others it is 'old rose'. *Immédiat* by L'Oréal or Wella's Koleston 2000 are less unpredictable where the precise tint is concerned.

Write for an hour every day. Anything. Even a letter to your local electricity company to tell them the light outside your house isn't working. You've no idea what an effect this daily exercise will have on your skin: that grimace at the corner of your mouth will disappear; the line where you knitted your brows will fade; your eyes will widen; and, with all this, inner peace will come.

I don't know whether you've noticed how incredibly young, energetic and radiant Nawal El Sadaawi, Hannaan al-Shaykh, Assia Djebar and

Liana Badr look, to name but a few. And the sheen of their hair, the sparkle in their eyes! Writing, I tell you, is a miracle the equal of all the revitalizing creams and energizing treatments.

Now, don't tell me my 'Writing = Elixir of Youth' theory fails to convince. I shan't believe you for a moment. And why not? Because I've tried both cream and writing, and writing, I tell you, works better!

It's the deepest, cheapest face-lift you can get in the Arab countries, where everything from the political regimes to the ideological pollution and economic climate conspire to make women old before their time, give them a nervous breakdown once a week, a heart attack once a month, white hair from the age of twenty-five and at least five wrinkles a year after twenty.

Like the women selling detergents, seen so often on our national TV screens, I recommend only what I test. I've been writing regularly for more than twenty years now, the way others do yoga or boxing, and I get compliments all the time: 'You look younger and younger! You're in good shape! How do you manage it?' Writing's my secret! Even to go and do battle with the grocer, who has (again!) slipped me three rotten pears in a kilo of five, I put the whole scene down on paper – what I'm going to say, what he'll reply. I analyse all the possible scenarios and write down my lines, keeping clear the essential point: I want three-fifths of my money back. Because that's what writing is: clarifying the essential point and getting it over, at all costs, to your opponent.

I'm sorry, I mean to your reader. Opponent is a very bad term since writing must not, above all, be confused with a boxing match.

In boxing, you land the blow directly on your enemy's nose. Wham! It's him or you. His nose against yours. (*Ahafid*! *Assatar*!). Writing is something else again. First, all those involved have to keep their noses intact – and that includes you. To write is to make an interlocutor of your opponent.

To write is to make someone who was indifferent into an attentive reader. This is, in fact, the whole secret of writing and what differentiates it from boxing. And it is what makes it work as a super revitalizing cream: the point is to turn the 'monsters' around you into adorable interlocutors who listen to you with delight. You don't even need to shout yourself hoarse to be listened to. Once you have learned to write – i.e. to get through some message close to your heart – the other person, previously indifferent, will now pay money to know what you have to say. Isn't this wonderful? It's an extraordinary discovery which Arab women ought to use at least as heavily as they use moisturizing cream!

But, you will say, how can monsters (and they make take the form of friends, colleagues, good Muslims, pleasant civil servants, etc.) be turned into attentive interlocutors? Well, that is where writing is much more effective than any elixir of youth or restorative exercises: first you have to transform yourself. Other people's interest is simply a consequence of that transformation. You have to believe, for example, that what you have to say is important and that, however fragile and insecure you might be, you have within you a little inner light (*shu'la*) worth heeding. If you want other people to stop being monsters who attack you as soon as you open your mouth to say something interesting and unique (of course!), you have to begin by giving up the boxer's posture. It took me years to understand that.

I began by writing articles that were vitriolic. That was in the 1970s in the now defunct monthly magazine *Lamalif*, administered and published, come hell or high water, by Zakia Daoud from Casablanca. Well, hell and high water did eventually get the better of the magazine, but that's another story. Let's stick to the cream and the boxing for now. People were shocked. Many of my friends and colleagues (often the same people) recognized themselves in the vile portraits, and acrimonious discussions ensued. Then, one day, I came to the conclusion that I really had to find a different method. What if I accentuated the positive, the things that were right, that gave hope, instead of getting bogged down in all that was wrong? Perhaps I would help myself – and others too – to see how you could wade on through the mire, and perhaps how you could avoid it – possibly even how you could learn to fly. And, anyway, what was there to lose from imagining a better world? This shift opened up to me incredible doors of friendship and comradeship and brought me harsh but constructive criticism and so much emotion, so many dreams and hopes reciprocated by readers of both sexes, giving me the boldness I needed to continue my explorations. Indeed now, if I am away from Rabat for ten days, I sink into a bottomless pit of homesickness. I have lost my anger along the way, or at least it is expressed in a different way.

To write, you have to let out your anger one way or another, or at least get on top of it, since putting it down on paper hardly solves the problem. I do not read a writer because she infuses me with anger; I read her because she spreads before me paths which explore a myriad inextricable ramifications of those little pent-up emotions and knotted affects which constitute anger, humiliation or frustration. All these familiar feelings which are the daily bread of all the people of the Maghreb, whatever their sex – but which are, particularly, the daily bread of women, for the simple reason that society is based, from the outset, on our silence. Accept and shut up. Not that men express themselves more, but they at least do not have to deal with their inferiority being regarded as sacred and trumpeted to the world as constitutive of their identity and specificity, as ours is in the codes of law which enjoin us to obey authority.

Authority is the key word where writing is concerned. Writing is one of the means human beings discovered thousands of years ago for challenging authority. You can shut yourself away quietly for an hour and write a long page to the Director of the Postal Services, who have just sent you something looking like the White House's phone bill for the Gulf War. That director is one of the most invisible personalities in the kingdom and getting through to him is as complicated as planning a pilgrimage to Mecca before the invention of the steam engine. Your letter may never arrive; but then again, it may, even if there is only one chance in a thousand. To write is to grasp this tiny, mini-mini-microscopic chance to express yourself. It is to take the risk of communicating with someone who doesn't give a damn for what you think and doesn't want to listen to you.

In this sense, it is an extraordinary opportunity for someone isolated, looked down on and excluded from decision-making to hold a dialogue with herself, first of all, then with her environment and, possibly, with the authorities. Of course, I can't guarantee you'll be read by anyone in authority, but what is certain is that, by making your daily attempt to express yourself, you will not so much change the world as change yourself. And I know that it is, in fact, by changing yourself that you change the world.

On this point, I shall be attacked by the politicos, most of whom feed us a diet of speeches intended to change us while they continue to peddle ossified programmes that have hardly changed for decades – indeed, not since the great independence years. Not that I deny the importance of political activism. There is, certainly, no substitute for it when it comes to communicating messages and transforming mentalities, but writing is of a different order and fulfils other functions.

There is, first of all, humility. The politician has a message to get through to you, a programme for changing your life. Like the *Résistance* cream the managing director of the cosmetics company wants to sell you. What you are being sold is something sure and certain. But writing (good writing, the sort that grabs you) is the act of a lost soul; the approach is that of someone fragile, who has no message, someone in search of herself, someone sure of nothing, except that something isn't right and it hurts.

Writing is an admission of impotence, but one reinforced and buttressed by an incredible generosity and marvellous faith in humanity and in its grandeur which derives from its being perfectible. Yes we, the people of the Maghreb, lost and anxious as we are, and ill at ease as we have so far been in this electronic century, can remake and reshape ourselves, transform and metamorphose ourselves, men and women, and take the place that is ours in a planet hurtling towards the galaxies of the future.

Writing is one of the most ancient forms of prayer. To write is to believe communication is possible, that other people are good, that you can make contact with their kindness, awaken their generosity and their desire to be better.

With that in mind, a group of women set up a writing workshop in May 1991 in Tunis. The idea of the workshop was a simple one: the Maghreb of the galaxies needs to know women's point of view. We have to learn to clarify our opinions, to refine our vision of ourselves and of the world around us. Not in order to dominate or show off, but simply to say quite plainly what we think. We can express ourselves in thousands of ways. Some people weave away in the shade at marvellous carpets; others embroider; others labour day and night in the factories; and, last of all, there are those who scratch away at paper in the chill offices of the civil service. A thousand ways of expressing themselves and contributing. The idea of the workshop was to break the monotony, to get together to help each other produce a book in many voices.

Yes, says the writer who takes up her pen each morning. We can recreate our little Maghreb in such a way as to reflect our wildest dreams. Yes, we can give this little Maghreb, which has neither enormous wealth, nor scientific laboratories, nor democratic experience, a little paradise of dialogue and understanding where each person, man or woman, leftist or fundamentalist, civil servant or student can come together, acknowledge each other's work and flourish, irrespective of differences.

It is this dream of a potentially other Maghreb which the members of the writing workshop, a collective fired with contradictory desires and buzzing with ideas, wanted, more or less, to share – first, among themselves, then with readers. The idea of the workshop emerged during the tragic days of the Gulf War. A telephone call from Tunis and the indefatigable Rachida En Naifar, with whom I am in constant dialogue, draws me out of my depression, explaining that the right to expression still remains the best way to fight for one's ideas. Why not share with the AFTURD group the experience acquired by the Moroccan research collectives which, after some failures, succeeded, with the aid of a publisher committed to the struggle for human rights (Leila Chaouni of the Éditions le Fennec), in producing several collections and more than eleven books.

In the plane taking me from Tunis to chair the workshop in May, I was suddenly seized with panic: how was a writing workshop to be successfully launched by three days' work when, in Morocco, it had taken hundreds of meetings, tens of altercations and scores of minor squabbles since 1984? I shall always remember the first collective, set up at the Law Faculty in Rabat with Professors Omar Azzimane, Aicha Belarbi, Aberrazzak Moulay Rachid, Fatema Zrioual, Moulay Ahmed Khamlichi and Alaoui Cherifa, to name but a few. The idea was to meet to spell out our vision of change together, to show how Morocco could be transformed, to offer alternatives. The hall was packed and there were teachers and students there who had come by train from Marrakesh and Fez. It was a touching sight: all these people wanting to come together to learn to express themselves. We started out in a stammering humility, only to end up, after some ten or so meetings, in disaster: politicos had decided to take over the group. They wanted us to agree on a 'platform'. But, as I repeated till I was blue in the face, how could we agree on a programme to change the world since I did not yet know what I wanted?

True writing is never a recipe. It is always a quest!

There never was a platform. That particular group collapsed because Morocco was undergoing some profound changes and the politicos carried on functioning in terms of 'programmes imposed from on high' instead of realizing that we were moving into a new phase of democratic atomization and freedom of expression. Four years later we started out again, but did so on such a humble basis that the majority were discouraged: everyone had to write thirty pages on what was regarded as a key theme. The first book in the 'Approches' series was born. The theme was 'Portraits of Women; Change and Resistance'. Those who wanted to seize power in the group realized there was no power to seize. No power, but articles to write. We did not see the authority-seekers again. The politicos who did contribute had already made a start on the new Morocco, the Morocco of tolerance and difference. We all learned a lot from this experience and many further collective works followed.

The secret of the success of collectives is not to get together to discuss everyone's political preferences, but to correct the titles and structures of articles. As for their content, since we believe in democracy, everyone is entitled to their own notions.

This was, in fact, what we tried to explore in the Tunis workshop, where we went through everything from pitched battles to moments of deep emotion, all of us subsiding at times into bouts of wild laughter. It was a space in which you could expose your weakness and fragility. There was no place there for the traditional pose of doing others down and showing what a great genius you were.

Everyone had a free hand in the choice of sub-theme they wanted to explore; they had only to convince the group of the connection with the overall theme. It was a fine thing to see Dorra Mahfoud Draoui explaining so very convincingly that cooking had a place in the analysis of ideology, and that the way we stuff our faces is every bit as much self-expression as the most highly crafted political speech.

I refer to Dorra's article, 'Cooking. Power and Women's Counter-power' not because it was the best, but because it is a good illustration of the idea of the freedom enjoyed by each member of the collective. The key idea in the workshop was that no-one was the best writer. We were not there for a boxing match, but to learn to express ourselves. I mention Dorra and her article to give a sense of what the resultant book was trying to do; it was neither a manifesto, nor a programme for women's liberation. That is a job for the ministers and all those whose duty it is to draw up forecasts and plans, in order to maximize our chances of starting out on new foundations.

The book was an invitation to join in some individual intellectual peregrinations, to follow some unusual lines of thought. It presents a series of different approaches to understanding, with reference to the specific Tunisian case, that inextricable knot of destiny which the Maghreb of tomorrow absolutely must unravel, a knot made by those threads – so entangled and entwined – which link 'women, ideologies and society'. Tunisia is one of the rare countries in the Arab world which made a choice, at a very early stage, to commit itself to modernity, with all that that entailed. It was a choice that has turned out to be full of risks and one which concerns us all since, alas, there is no other course for this dear Arab world than to embrace its century. Even if we suffer a little in the process.

So hang on tight now, particularly to your pen, since there are those who would grab it from you! Happy reading! And don't forget the idea we began with: writing is better than skin cream!

Notes

This chapter was first published as the introduction to *Femmes, Idéologies et Société en Tunisie* (the book resulting from a workshop held in Tunis in the Summer of 1991) (n.pub., n.d.)

1. One dirham is roughly 50p.

CHAPTER II

Rebuild Baghdad?
But in What Galaxy?

An American sociologist passing through Rabat told me in May 1991 that he was surprised to find no one in the city talking about the Gulf War. It was 'as if it had never happened', he added. I in turn was surprised to hear myself reply that it was a good thing the Arabs were keeping quiet, since they had, for once, understood that it is by and through action that a future is shaped. And, in my view, the most important lesson this war has taught is that the highest of solitudes, to borrow Taher Ben Jalloun's phrase, is not that of an illiterate and penniless Arab man or woman, however deprived they may be. More alone and more fragile than a humiliated Arab people is an Arab leader with only the external trappings of power.

Lonely and fragile are our leaders! Sometimes, watching the television, I was choking back the tears. Beneath their more or less well affixed masks, they reflected our impotence and despair. And did so, indeed, whichever side they had chosen: for or against America.

The great revelation of this war and, for me, the revelation which heralds 21st-century Arab power as a more attainable goal than we had previously thought, is that the Arab leaders are doomed to share the same destiny as their peoples. This war has wiped out the historical distance between a potent leader and an eternally castrated people. And this is the only thing that could legitimate – or at least justify – the Iraqi deaths, including the deaths of many children. May they at least become the sacrificial victims of a democracy yet to be built.

A strong Arab leader can never exist without a strong Arab people. And, in contrast to the way we thought before this war, the strength of a people has nothing to do with the idiocy of arms. A strong people is a people with education and high technology skills, not a people sitting on tons of ammunition with their fingers on the trigger. And this is true whether the intended victim is internal or external.

The American army did not defeat the Arab army because it had greater firepower. We would do well to understand this since our whole future depends on it. The American army defeated the Arab army for at least two reasons: the democratization of decision-making power and the access of the large mass of the population to knowledge. The American army is an army of all creeds and colours, which is educated and rendered responsible by a rational distribution of tasks and decision-making. It is highly significant that on the Iraqi side the whole of the political stage was occupied by just a single will, that of the unique, irreplaceable Saddam Hussein and his faithful, obedient messenger, Mr. Aeroplane – Tariq Aziz.

The strength of America – as compared with Arab impotence – with its political stage where divergences and dissonant opinions are displayed for all to see and there is recourse to secrecy and censorship only when all parties agree, lies, among other things, in the fact that America's soldiers, from the privates to the general, were born into the laps of literate little mothers.

And don't, for the love of heaven, start jumping up and down and telling me the opposite is true, though you'll surely find the arguments to do so. Obviously, you could dismiss what I say by arguing that quality education in the USA is reserved for the moneyed elite, that it is private, that blacks are kept out and so on. And, what's more, you'd be right! But in spite of the blatant inequalities in the American system, knowledge is more accessible to the masses and decision-making more widely shared: two facts which mean that the American brain functions with fewer fetters than those which shackle and paralyse its Arab counterpart. That is the key fact and it shows us the path to follow. Go on with your old archaic, outdated nationalism. I am not singing the praises of America to humiliate us even more. I am trying, in spite of all the pain which torments me and suffocates you, to see what constitutes the strength of a nation at the dawn of the 21st century. The democratization of knowledge and decision-making is the path which leads to that strength.

Listen to me, because I am speaking out of my pain and my humiliation. The arrogant Fatima died the night Baghdad was attacked by a fire beyond the Mongols' imagining. A fire reflected on millions of television screens where Iraqi death was turned into entertainment. A spectacle of such limpid cruelty that it made that of the Roman gladiators, whom the emperors used to feed to the lions, seem a sweet little diversion.

The only Arab world worthy of being fought for and worth clashing over in our discussions is one in which the Arab brain can extend its capacities the way a free bird extends its wings to reach the heights. And that Arab world can only exist if – and on condition that – the chief educator of the brain also shares in this modern technological knowledge. And that chief educator is, I tell you, neither the army of educational experts (schoolteachers and university professors), nor the civil servants in the ministries of education and national culture. That chief educator is woman, who, as mother, nourishes the child, in the fateful first five years, with the knowledge she possesses.

The lesson of the Gulf War, a lesson you, the leaders of the Arab countries, will read in no Western document, is that the mother of all battles (*umm al-maa'rik*) is not the one you fight against the Americans, but the one you fight against illiteracy – the illiteracy of men and women. But, up to now, the impression has been that the budgets of the national education ministries are only for men. Thirty years after independence, 90% of Moroccan women in rural areas are illiterate and 100% of them politically marginalized. You will never be powerful, Mr. Arab leader, in a modern world where democratized and democratizing knowledge is both arm and ammunition. You will never be anything but backward outsiders in the world of satellite-borne information, whilst your mothers, sisters, wives and, most importantly, your secretaries, maids and women workers are illiterate. I omitted your daughters from the list because we all know an Arab man is hugely committed to the education of his daughter. She is the only woman with whom he identifies and whose future causes him concern. But we shall all, men and women, leave behind the mutilating law of the tribe-family and take our first steps in the space and planetary age the moment we realize that our destiny is linked to the most deprived, the most excluded of all: the poor woman, ground down in field and factory, on whom any arbitrary power whatever may be visited. The subjugated, scorned and humiliated Arab will be transformed into an autonomous, self-governing person the day he is suckled by an autonomous mother. And the path to the autonomy of the individual is through access to worthwhile knowledge. The day the political leader understands that the most faithful mirror to his strength is the reflection which comes back to him from the female citizens living in the remotest villages, the planetary Arab will be born.

An Arab at ease in the galaxies, interested in their movements and attuned to their secrets, can only be born of a woman who weaves her ideas around the satellite networks with the ease with which her ancestors wove a thousand geometrical flowers into their carpets.

When we realize that the strength of the leader consists neither in the weakness of the people nor in the exclusion of women, then will be born that magnificent being we all desire so intensely – the planetary Arab. The value of such individuals will depend neither on their sex, nor on their position in the hierarchy, but on their glorious humanity. And there, Sirs, the Arabs will need neither *umm al-maa'rik* nor *ab al-hurub* (the father of all wars) to display and test out their power. It will unfold with human gentleness and tranquil dignity.

So saying, gentlemen, I shall leave you in the presence of *Chahrazad n'est pas marocaine* (Sheherezade is not Moroccan). Leila Chaouni, the publisher, has decided to bring out a new edition of this book, out of print since well before the war, in response to the requests of readers – male and female. I have puzzled over the reasons for the continued interest of those readers in a book no foreign publisher wanted to translate – unlike my other books, which the Turks, Pakistanis, Spaniards and Germans translated so eagerly. Re-reading *Chahrazad* three years later, I realize its message is an intrinsically Moroccan one. It is an intimist monologue. Just between ourselves. Like the confidences of a summer night in Morocco. The dark beauty of those nights is so special, so profound that it lowers our defences. Perhaps it is the fact that the book was written during summer nights on an isolated beach after an unhappy love-affair that gives it its character, which is so hermetically Moroccan, or perhaps it is its message, as simple as it is inescapable: archaism is the product of the exclusion of women from knowledge. This is no longer of any moment, which is well and good, and it is good that it should now even have become, essentially, embarrassing. And, since I know that all Moroccans have a head for business (*tbarkalah 'alihum*), I know they will carefully weigh up the facts and figures I advance to show that the illiterate woman can no longer make any contribution either to field or factory, since the feast to which we are invited today – with all the other inhabitants of the planet – is the feast of knowledge:

> Knowledge itself, therefore, turns out to be not only the source of the highest-quality power, but also the most important ingredient of force and wealth. Put differently, knowledge has gone from being an adjunct of money power and muscle power to being their very essence. It is, in fact, the ultimate amplifier. This is the key to the powershift that lies ahead, and it explains why the battle for control of knowledge and the means of communication is heating up all over the world.[1]

This is Mr. Alvin Toffler speaking, prophet of the American future, which, inevitably, is ours too, as we wait for King Schahriah to reawaken.

Wa adraka Chahrazad as-sabah
fa-nadarat ila al-gamar al-listina'i al-mubah.[2]

Notes

This chapter was originally published as the Introduction to the second edition of *Chahrazad n'est pas Marocaine. Autrement elle serait salariée!*

1. Alvin Toffler, *Powershift: Knowledge, Affluence and Power in the 21st Century* (Düsseldorf, Vienna, New York: Econ., 1991), p.40.

2. Mernissian reformulation of the ritual phrase which punctuates the *Thousand and One Nights*: 'Morning surprised Sheherezade, and she fixed her eyes on the permitted TV satellite dish.' Naturally, granting permission to speak (*al-kalam al-mubah*) is no longer today the privilege of King Schahriah of the Arabs, but of the boss of CNN.

CHAPTER III

Morocco:
The Merchant's Daughter
and the Son of the Sultan

Revolution is to understand the other's unfamiliar and threatening languages.

'Feminism is not home-grown in Arab lands, it is an import from Western capitals.' This often-heard statement is shared by two groups of people one would never think of as having anything in common: Conservative Religious Arab Male Leaders, and the Provincial Western Feminists. The implication of this statement is that the Arab woman is a semi-idiotic submissive subhuman who bathes happily in patriarchally organized degradation and institutionalized deprivation.

With the first group – the conservative religious Arab male leaders – one can immediately identify the interests lying behind such a vision of the Arab woman. The statement itself reflects a key ideological assumption necessary if patriarchal Islam is to exist and thrive at all. A rebellious Arab female has been identified since the dawn of Islam as a potent threat. Quotes from the prestigious Bukhari's Hadith, where women are equated with social disorder, and with Satan, were piously repeated to me when I showed any dissenting initiative, even at age six.

In the Qur'an there are two concepts referring to female subversive drives and disruptive powers: *nushuz* and *qaid*. Both refer to woman's potential for being an uncooperative and unreliable citizen of the Moslem *umma* (community). *nushuz* refers specifically to the wife's rebellious tendencies toward her husband in an area where female obedience is vital: sexuality. The Qur'an calls *nushuz* the wife's decision not to comply with her husband's desire to have intercourse. *Qaid* is the key word in the Sura of Joseph, where the handsome prophet was harassed by an unscrupulous and persevering adulterous wife. Despite the sacred stamp the Qur'an itself branded onto female subversive potential in the 7th century, contemporary male Arab leaders open big eyes and scream about Western destructive imported ideas whenever they sense any rebellion on the part of Arab women. The attitude of these men is understandable: if they acknowledge that women's resistance to patriarchal Islam is an *indigenous* phenomenon, they will have to face the fact that aggression against their system has come not only from Washington and Paris but also from the women they embrace every night. Who wants to live with such a thought?

The Qur'an – like the sacred texts of the two other great monotheistic religions Islam claims as reference and source (Judaism and Christianity) – proffers models of hierarchical relationships and sexual inequality. These models have been underscored for fourteen centuries by various additional elements, including the Muslim Golden Age of triumph and of political/economic power, during which time the concept of the *jawari* (or highly accomplished, learned, exquisite female pleasure slaves) came into being. This is the fabricated archetype that Arab and Muslim women must confront. The *jawari*, who were given as gifts (and bribes and rewards) among powerful men, were the secular aspect of what the Qur'an describes as the houri, the eternally virgin, loving, and beautiful female creature offered as a reward in paradise to devout believers – devour *male* believers, that is. These sacred and secular models of woman have had enormous influence on the creation and maintenance of sex roles in Muslim civilization. Why *wouldn't* women rebel?

The reality of the Arab woman's life is not, after all, out of the *Arabian Nights*, much as many Arab men and most Western tourists would like to believe. The reality of most Moroccan women's lives, for instance, consists of enormous and vital (but often unacknowledged) labour: carpet-weaving, bead-setting, leather embroidery, sewing, fieldwork in agriculture, jobs in the massive bureaucratic administration, in light industry, and – of course – in the service sector and in housework, cooking, and childcare.

Colonization, to be sure, devalued women's labour even further than the indigenous patriarchal systems had, and with a double effect: the downgrading of manual labour in contrast to technical expertise, and the specific downgrading of *domestic* labour within the capitalist concept that defines domestic labour as nonproductive and therefore doesn't stoop to integrate it into national accounts.

Nationalization – for all its tragic and repeated historical betrayals of women (as in Algeria) – is nonetheless a strong determining factor in shaping women's expectations. For example, the North African woman of today usually dreams of having a steady, wage-paying job with social security and health and retirement benefits, at a state institution; these women don't look to a man any longer for their survival, but to the state. While perhaps not ideal, this is nevertheless a breakthrough, an erosion of tradition. It also partly explains Moroccan women's active participation in the urbanization process: they are leaving rural areas in numbers equalling men's migrations, for a 'better life' in the cities – and in *European* cities, as well. The rate of women's participation in activities outside of the kingdom's territory is 40 per cent, according to a recent employment survey.[1]

Furthermore, women's participation in various professions is growing[2] surprisingly high, even if one considers that until World War II Moroccan women were kept secluded and prevented from attending schools or competing for diplomas and jobs in both private and public sectors. Their contributions to agriculture, crafts, and services were limited to traditional spaces and were masked behind their domestic identity. They contributed as wives, mothers, daughters, aunts – but not as women *per se*.

But if Moroccan women in the 1940s and 1950s accepted domestic work as fate, younger women today aspire to education and jobs. And it is still very difficult for them. In bureaucratic and industrial employment areas, it is only the woman with two or more years of secondary education who has a chance, and then only after obtaining secretarial skills. In 1982, only 37.4 per cent of primary school, 33.1 per cent of secondary school and 26.3 per cent of university enrolments were female.

When this chapter was first written, Morocco was preparing for a highly irregular event: elections. At the previous elections (1977), women voters numbered 3 million. Among 906 candidates for parliament, eight were women – and none were elected. Our actual parliament is all male. But today women constitute almost half of the electorate – and that's what matters to the political parties, who were outdoing each other in trying to manipulate female voters and win them over. For these brief weeks, we Moroccan women were living in an incredible time-space, where male politicians, usually oblivious to women's needs, were trying to find a convincing language for actually talking to women. They needed to accomplish miracles to find the right tone, because they had to renounce their centuries-old prejudices. They needed to overcome their stereotypes of femininity/passivity and open their eyes to the reality of Moroccan women, whose main worries are not, after all, make-up, veiling, and belly dancing, but having equal opportunities in education, employment, promotion, etc.

In light of all this, the belief on the part of some Western feminists that Arab women are subservient, obedient slaves, who discovered consciousness-raising and illuminating revolutionary ideas only when fed such goodies by the most liberated of all women (New York, Paris and London feminists), is less understandable at first sight than the utterance of such sentiments by Arab patriarchs. But if you carefully ask yourself (as I often have) why an American or French feminist will think that I am less clever than she in grasping patriarchal degradation schemes, you realize that it gives her an immediate control of the situation; she is the leader and I the follower. She, in spite of her claimed desire to change the system and make it more egalitarian for women, retains (lurking deep down in her subliminal ideological genes) the racist and imperialist Western *male* distorting drives. Even when faced with an Arab woman who has similar diplomas, knowledge, and experience, she unconsciously reproduces the supremacist colonial pattern. Every time I come across a Western feminist who thinks that I am indebted to her for my own development on feminist issues, I worry not so much about the prospects of an international sisterhood, but about the possibility of Western feminism's transforming itself into popular social movements able to produce structural change in the world centres of industrialized empires. The basic question for each woman who thinks herself a feminist is not how far ahead she is in her consciousness compared to women from other cultures, but how much she *shares* in that consciousness with women from different social classes in her *own* society. Sisterhood will be global when it cuts through both class and culture.

One of the steps necessary for intellectual women to share their privileged access to knowledge and higher consciousness is to try to decipher women's refutation of patriarchy when voiced in languages other than their own. One such endeavour is to grasp and decode illiterate women's rebellion, whether voiced in oral culture or in specifically dissenting practices considered marginal, criminal, or erratic. One of my greatest lessons in humility is the one I received from listening closely to folk tales told by my illiterate Aunt Aziza, who is now seventy-nine years old. One of them goes as follows:

The Merchant's Daughter and the Son of the Sultan[3]

A rich merchant possessed a daughter named A'isha, as lovely as the moon. (Sing praises to God who created such a beautiful image.) One evening, while she was taking a stroll on her roof-top terrace, as was her custom, her nurse presented her with a bowl of soup of *mhamça*. In drinking her soup, she let spill on her breast a small pastry ball which she proceeded to bring again to her mouth. On the adjoining terrace, the son of the Sultan saw her and said,

'O Lalla who tends basil and waters her crop on her terrace, I beg you to tell me how many leaves there are to your plant.'

'O Son of the Sultan,' she replied, 'you who reign over vast lands, O learned one, you a doctor who reads the Qur'an, tell me how many fish there are in the sea, stars in the heavens, dots in the Qur'an.'[4]

'Be quiet greedy one,' he mocked. 'You have taken the *mhamça* spilled on your breast and have eaten it.'

The young girl descended from the terrace very displeased and asked her nurse to accompany her to the sanctuary of Moulay Idrise so that she might be entertained there and clear her mind. In making her way, she once again came upon the son of the Sultan. This time he was seated close by a vendor of fruits, eating a pomegranate. One seed from this pomegranate fell to the ground between his *balghas*[5] and he picked it up again and ate it. The young woman was gleeful to have witnessed this surprise gesture on his part and returned to her home in very fine spirits indeed.

Early the next morning, as usual, she climbed to her terrace and watered her pot of basil and worked on her embroidery. Later, the two young people engaged in the same dialogue that had taken place the night before:

'O Lalla who tends her basil, how many leaves are there to your plant?'

'O Son of the Sultan, you who reign over vast lands, O learned one, you a doctor who reads the Qur'an, tell me how many fish there are in the sea, stars in the heavens, and dots in the Qur'an.'

'Go along with you, O covetous one, you who took the *mhamça* spilled on your breast and have eaten it again.'

But this time, on hearing these words, the young woman triumphantly replied, 'Go along with you, O covetous one, who reclaimed the pomegranate seed that fell to the mud between your *balghas* and ate it again.'

This turn of events prompted the prince to leave in a very vexed state. He purchased clothing to disguise himself as a travelling vendor of women's wares. Hooded in black, with black *balghas*, and carrying his wares, he went through the streets crying out all the way to the residence of the daughter of the merchant. 'Perfume!' he shouted, 'Mirrors! Towels! Combs! Rings!' So good was his imitation that she took him to be a true vendor and sent her Dada to buy her some perfume. Seeing that his ruse was working, the disguised prince said to the Dada,

'Choose and take all that you desire. For all that I have, all I ask is for a kiss on the cheek from your mistress.' The merchant's daughter consented to this and kissed the sooty merchant on the cheek. He then departed wholly satisfied at his success.

The next day, he went up to his terrace and found her watering her basil. Their usual dialogue took place. But this time, the prince triumphed with a retort:

'I posed as a street vendor and dallied with the cheek of the daughter of a merchant.' Covered with confusion, Lalla A'isha recounted to her aunt all that had taken place and asked for help in being skilfully disguised so that she might appear as a slave. Changed for all appearances sake, she was led to the slave market by her aunt and sold. The slave trader found the girl so beautiful that he offered her to the son of the Sultan and sent her to him. Lalla A'isha brought with her a razor, a cucumber, rouge, and a very strong sleeping potion. She gave the prince this potion and when he had fallen asleep, she shaved off his beard and moustache, made him up to be a woman, hung a mirror around his neck, stuck a cucumber up his anus, and ran off. On returning home, she carefully washed herself and dressed in her own garments, while the prince was awakening to find himself in totally humiliating circumstances.

The next morning, on the roof-top terrace, the usual dialogue took place between the young woman and the prince (now sporting the silky skin of a woman). This time, she was able to end the conversation victoriously:

'I posed as a slave and played many a deceitful trick on a prince.'

Furious and humiliated, the son of the Sultan swore that he would marry this opinionated young creature and force her to acknowledge that man is more cunning than woman. He asked for her hand in marriage, and this was granted by her father. Once she was in his possession, he incarcerated her in an underground cell, giving her only large, baggy garments to wear and barley bread once daily with a pitcher of Wad water[6] to drink.

But the sly young woman dug an underground tunnel allowing her to be in touch with her parents' household. There she would go every day to eat and drink, taking care to return to the cell for those times when her husband appeared to replenish her supplies. In handing her the black bread and pitcher, he would say:

'Lalla A'isha, the sorry inhabitant of the cell, who is the shrewdest, man or woman?'

'A woman, my Lord,' was her reply. He was unable to make her surrender.

Days passed in this fashion. The Sultan died and his son succeeded him. At the beginning of spring, the young Sultan decided to spend some time in the country, as was his usual custom, and he went first to visit his wife in the cell.

'In eight days,' he told her, 'at five in the morning, I am leaving for Sour, where I will stay for about fifteen days.'

'Enjoy yourself!' replied the young woman. 'May you have luck.' And she eagerly went by the underground tunnel to her father's, where she asked that she be provided with more sumptuous provisions and trappings than the Sultan himself would have at Sour. She wished to be comfortably settled there before he was to arrive.

The night before his departure, the Sultan went to bid his wife farewell, and the following day at dawn he started on his journey. When he arrived at Sour, he noticed tents of a much finer velvet than his own. Positioned at one of the tents was a young slave, beautifully attired. Very surprised, he made inquiries and learned that an exquisite young woman had come that same morning for a stay of several days. Full of curiosity, he told the slave to ask her mistress if she would receive him. She replied that her mistress said no one could see her who had not spent the three previous days in the town as a *farnatchi*, collecting horse-dung.

The Sultan complied and returned three days later. Water was heated so that he might bathe and dress finely, and he was now allowed into the tent of the mysterious woman.

'I will not talk with you,' stated Lalla A'isha, 'unless you agree to a contract of marriage; and that I may have your sword and belt as a dowry.' Touched by the sweetness of this voice, the Sultan agreed. Without realizing how much time was passing, he spent twenty full days with his beloved without recognizing her. On the twentieth day, they came and told him that if he did not return a revolution would unleash itself. So he left. His wife had become pregnant.

By the time the Sultan returned home, Lalla A'isha had already re-entered the cell. The first thing he did in going to see her was to persuade her to acknowledge the superiority of man's cleverness over woman's. 'I stayed,' he told her, 'twenty delicious and delightful days with a woman with your eyes, your hands, your figure, and a voice like your own.'

'In truth, your fortune is large and you are not short on good luck coming your way. Joy and pleasure be with you!' she replied contentedly.

And all continued as it had before. In her fifth month of pregnancy, Lalla A'isha began preparations for the birth of her child. In the ninth month, she into the world brought a boy, whom she named Sour.

The following spring, the Sultan went again to the country, choosing to erect his tents in a place called Dour. Lalla A'isha preceded his arrival as she had the year before, and all passed in similar fashion. This time she demanded that the Sultan spend three days as a vendor of condiments, and give her as dowry his sheath with its silk cord. Later, she gave birth to a second child, whom she named Dour.

The third year, events passed in the same fashion at El Qcour. On this occasion the Sultan had to spend three days cleaning the tent that housed the beautiful woman's horse and give her his ring as dowry. The child born this time was a girl, who received the name of Lalla Hamameh El Qcour, the dove of palaces.

Each time he came by the cell, Lalla A'isha refused to acknowledge to her husband the superiority of men over women. The Sultan reached the point where he had had enough of this obstinate woman. He told her that he intended to take a new wife, who would be his favourite. She acquiesced, unmoved.

'To Allah, may you triumph and strengthen your reign!' she said. 'When are they going to prepare the chamber for the new spouse?'

'On such a day as this,' he replied.

'Very good. I wish you good luck.'

On the designated day, she dressed her children in their best clothes. She led them to the palace and ordered them to help with the nuptials. The children carried out this task marvellously, ransacking everything. When they were chased out they cried: 'This house is the home of our father and those who chase us are the sons of dogs, they cried out as loud as they could.

'Come my brother Sour! Come my brother Dour! Come my sister Lalla Hamameh El Qcour!'

The Sultan thus learned that these were his children, and he had to acknowledge that woman is much cleverer than man. He dismissed the idea of marrying any other woman, and it was in Lalla A'isha's honour that the celebrations were carried out.

If they have not yet done feasting, they must be at it still.

Notes

1. Direction de la Statistique, 1979, Rabat.

2. Except for the areas of trade and business, Moroccan women have managed to set foot in practically all spheres, including the previously highly male world of '*professions libérales et scientifiques*'. They constitute 30 percent of that body; 16.9 percent of university teachers, one quarter of secondary-school teachers, and one-third of primary-school teachers are women.

3. Based on a translation by Lila Heron.

4. The Qur'an is written in the Arabic alphabet, which includes many letters which have dots as constitutive components.

5. Loose trousers.

6. Unprocessed river water not fit for drinking.

CHAPTER IV

Women, Saints, and Sanctuaries

The next morning I went to see my mother. I had a snack with her
and the children and then I went to spend the day at the Marabout
(sanctuary).[1] I lay down there and slept for a very long time.

Do you go to the Marabout often?
Yes, quite often. For example I prefer to go there on the days of *Aïd*
[religious festivals]. When one has a family as desperate as mine, the
shrine is a haven of peace and quiet. I like to go there.

What is it you like about the shrine? Can you be more precise?
Yes. The silence, the carpets, and the clean mats which are nicely
arranged . . . the sound of the fountain in the silence. An enormous
silence where the sound of water is as fragile as thread. I stay there
hours, sometimes whole days.

The day of Aïd *it must be full of people.*
Yes, there are people, but they are lost in their own problems. So they
leave you alone. Mostly it's women who cry without speaking, each
in her own world.

Aren't there any men at the shrine?
Yes, but the men have their side, and the women theirs. Men come
to visit the shrine and leave very quickly; the women, especially those
with problems, stay much longer.

What do they do and what do they say?
That depends. Some are happy just to cry. Others take hold of the
saint's garments and say, 'Give me this, oh saint, give me that. . . . I
want my daughter to pass her exam . . .' [she laughs]. You know the
saints are men, human beings. But sometimes, imagine, the woman
gets what she asks for! Then she brings a sacrifice, she kills an animal
and prepares a meal of the meat and then offers it to the visitors. Do
you know Sid El Gomri?

No.

[laughs] Salé is full of shrines . . . full, full. You know, there is a proverb, 'If you want to make a pilgrimage, just go around Salé barefoot. . .' [laughs]. They do say that . . . All of Salé is a shrine. There are so many that some don't have names [laughs]. My father is a native of Salé. He knows the shrines and talks a lot about them. When you are separated from someone or when you have a very bad fight, the saint helps you overcome your problem. When I go I listen to the women. You see them telling everything to the tomb and mimicking all that took place. Then they ask Sid El Gomri to help them get out of the mess. They cry, they scream. Then they get hold of themselves and come back, join us, and sit in silence. I like the shrine.

Are you ever afraid?
Afraid of what? In a shrine, what a question? I love shrines.

And when do you go?
They are shut in the evenings except for those that have rooms, like Sidi Ben Achir, for example. You can rent a room there and you can stay a long time.

Rent a room for how much?
Oh, fifteen dirhams.[2]

Fifteen dirhams a night?!
No, for ten dirhams you can stay as long as you like, even a month. You know, they call Sidi Ben Achir a healer. Sick people come with their family; they rent a room and stay until they are well. You know, it's not Sidi Ben Achir that cures them, it's God, but they think it's Sidi Ben Achir.

Can anybody rent a room?
Not any more. Now you have to have the authorization of the *mokhadem* [local official]. They want to know where you live and be sure that you are really sick. Once a woman rented a room and told them she had a sick person, but it was her lover. Since then they've made renting rooms more difficult.

Are there young people your own age at the shrine?
Yes, but they don't come for the shrine, only for the view. A lot of young men from the neighbourhood come to the shrine for picnics

during the spring and summer. You should see the shrine then – the Hondas, the motors roaring, the boys all dressed up, the girls with short skirts, all made up and suntanned. It's beautiful. It's relaxing . . . the silence inside of the shrine, and life outside . . . it's crawling with young people. You know they have even made a slide on the wall that goes down to the beach. I will show it to you when we go. It's faster. You jump off the rampart, go down the slide and you're on the beach. You know, some people come to the shrine in the summer for their holidays instead of going to a hotel which costs ten or fifteen dirhams a day. In the shrine a whole family pays fifteen or twenty dirhams a week or month. It's especially the people who don't live in the city and come from far away, the north, the south, all corners of Morocco. For them the shrine is ideal for holidays. The old people can pray and the young can go to the beach. In the summer I meet people from all over Morocco. It's as if I were in Mecca, but I'm in Salé! You must come and see it. We can go in the summer if you want, it's more pleasant. You don't have to come to pray, you can just come and look. I told you, when I go to the shrine it's not to pray. I never ask for anything. When I want something I'll ask God directly, but not the saint – he's a human being like I am.

This excerpt from an interview with a twenty-year-old maid, who works in a luxurious, modern part of Salé and lives in its *bidonville* section, suggests the great variety of experiences which take place in the sanctuary according to individual needs. Although they vary throughout the Maghreb from a humble pyramid of stones to a pretentious palace-like building,[3] all sanctuaries have one element in common: the saint's presence is supposed to be hosted there, because it is his tomb, a place he inhabited, or the site of an event in his life. The sanctuary testifies to the saint's welcome presence in the community, but as an institution in a dynamic developing society it also reflects the society's economic and ideological contradictions.

Sanctuaries as Therapy

For women, the sanctuary offers a dramatic contrast to their subordinate position in a bureaucratic, patriarchal society where decision-making positions are held by men. In the courts and hospitals, women hold a classically powerless position, condemned to be subjects, receptacles of impersonal decisions, executors of orders given by males. In a public hospital, the doctor is the expert, the representative of the bureaucratic order, empowered by the written law to tell her what to do; the illiterate woman can only execute his orders. In the diagnosis process, she expresses her discomfort in awkward colloquial Arabic and realizes, because of the doctor's impatience and irritation, that she cannot provide him with the precise, technical information he needs. Moreover, the hospital is a strange, alien setting, a modern building full of enigmatic written signs on doors and corridors, white-robed, clean and arrogant civil servants who speak French for all important communications and use Arabic only to issue elementary orders (come here, go there, take off your dress, etc.).

In comparison to the guardians who stand at the hospital gates and offices, the saint's tomb is directly accessible to troubled persons. Holding the saint's symbolic drape or some other object, like a stone or a tree, the woman describes what ails her, and it is she who makes the diagnosis, suggests the solution or solutions which might suit her, and explains to the saint the one she prefers. Saints know no French and often no literate Arabic; the language of this supernatural world is colloquial dialect Berber or Arabic – the only ones women master. The task of the saint is to help her reach her goal. She will give him a gift or a sacrifice only if he realizes her wishes, not before. With a doctor, she has to buy the prescription first and has no way of retaliating if the medicine does not have the proper effect. It is no wonder, then, that in spite of modern health services, women still go to the sanctuaries in swarms, before they go to the hospital, or simultaneously, or after. Saints give women vital help that modern public health services cannot give. They embody the refusal to accept arrogant expertise, to submit blindly to authority, to be treated as subordinate. This insistence on going to saints' tombs exemplifies the North African woman's traditional claim that she is active, can decide her needs for herself and do something about them, a claim that the Muslim patriarchal system denies her. Visits to and involvement with saints and sanctuaries are two of the rare options left to women to *be*, to shape their world and their lives. And this attempt at self-determination takes the form of an exclusively female collective endeavour.

In the sanctuaries, there are always more women than men. They speak and shout with loud voices as if they are the secure owners of the premises. Men, although allowed in, often have to shorten their *ziara* (visit) because they are overwhelmed by the inquisitive and curious looks of ubiquitous female visitors. Women gather around each other at the saint's supposed tomb and feel directly in contact with the sacred source of power that reflects their own energies. Distressed and suffering, these women have a very important bond: the will to find a solution, to find a happier balance between themselves and their surroundings, their fate, the system that thwarts them. They know they are wronged (*madluma*) by the system. Their desire to find an answer to their urgent needs is a desire to regain their rights. That other women are in exactly the same situation creates a therapeutic network of communication among them.

When a woman enters the sanctuary, she goes directly to the tomb, walking over the stretched feet of sitting women, the stretched bodies of sleeping women. If women have already cried and screamed, they often lie in a foetal position with their heads on the floor. The newly arrived woman will put her hand on the tomb, or on the drape over it, and will explain her problem either in a loud voice or silently. She might go into great detail about her son who failed his examination or was driven away from her by his bride. When describing an intimate fight with her husband, the woman will mimic what happened, name the actors, explain their gestures and attitudes. After she has expressed her needs, she will come to sit among the other women. Eventually, they will gather around her, ask her more details, and offer her the only expertise these women have: experience in suffering. Outraged by her situation and encouraged by this female community, the woman may fall on the floor and scream, twisting her body violently. Some women will rush to her, hold her, hug her, soothe her by talking to her about their own cases and problems. They will massage her forehead, cool her off with a drink of water, and replace on her head her displaced headgear or scarf. She recovers quickly, regains her composure; and leaves the scene to the next newcomer. Undeniably therapeutic, the sanctuary stimulates the energies of women against their discontent and allows them to bathe in an intrinsically female community of soothers, supporters and advisers.

Sanctuaries as Anti-establishment Arenas

It is primarily as an informal women's association that the sanctuary must be viewed. It is not a religious space, as is often mistakenly believed. Most saints' sanctuaries are not mosques. With very few exceptions, they are not places where official orthodox Muslim prayer takes place. As Derminghem remarks, 'In principal, the *kubba* is not a mosque (*masjid*) where one does *soujoud*, the prostration of ritual prayer (*sala*), even less so, the *jami'a*, the cathedral mosque where Friday service is held. One can do the *dou'a*, a prayer of supplication and optional invocation, but not the *sala*, sacramental prayer before a grave.'[4] The institution of saints that is enacted in the sanctuary has an evident anti-orthodox, anti-establishment component which has been the object of a prolific literature. But studies of the woman–saint relation have placed excessive emphasis on its magical aspect. Western scholars who investigated the institution were fascinated by the 'paralogical' component of the 'Moroccan personality structure' and the importance of magical thinking patterns in the still heavily agrarian Moroccan economy and paid little attention to what I would call the phenomenological aspect, namely, what the practitioners themselves derive from their involvement with the saint and the sanctuary.

Such practices have also been interpreted as evidence of the mystical thinking of primitives as opposed to the secularity of the modern mind. As Mary Douglas points out,

> Secularization is often treated as a modern trend attributable to the growth of cities or to the prestige of science, or just to the old breakdown of social forms. But we shall see that it is an age-old cosmological type, a product of a definable social experience, which need have nothing to do with urban life or modern science. Here it would seem that anthropology has failed to hold up the right reflecting mirror to contemporary man. The contrast of secular with religious has nothing whatever to do with the contrast of modern with traditional or primitive. The idea that primitive man is by nature deeply religious is nonsense. . . . The illusion that all primitives are pious, credulous and subject to the teaching of priests or magicians has probably done even more to impede our understanding of our civilization.[5]

Women, in particular, who are always the ones to be kept illiterate (and 97 per cent of rural Moroccan women still are),[6] are described as simple-minded, superstitious creatures, incapable of sophisticated thinking, who indulge in esoteric mysticism. This view of women has gained even greater support with the advent of the development and nascent industrialization of Third World economies. If women in industrialized societies are granted some capacity for rational thinking, women in Third World societies are still described as enthralled in magical thinking, despite the fact that their societies are leaping into a modernity enraptured with rationality, technology, and environmental mastery.

Sainthood as an Alternative to Male-defined Femininity

Far from magical, a visit to a saint's tomb, an ongoing relation with a supernatural creature, can be a genuine attempt to mediate one's place in the material world. Interaction with the saint can represent an effort to experience reality fully: 'The sacred is the real *par excellence*, at one and the same time power, efficiency, source of life and fertility. The religious desire to live within the sacred is in fact equivalent to the desire to be in objective reality, not to be paralysed by endless and purely subjective experience, but to live in a world which is real and efficient, and not illusory.'[7]

At bottom, women in an unflinchingly patriarchal society seek through the saint's mediation a bigger share of power, of control. One area in which they seek almost total control is reproduction and sexuality, the central notions of any patriarchal system's definition of women, classical orthodox Islam included.[8] Women who are desperate to find husbands, women whose husbands have sexual problems, women who have lost their husband's love or their own reproductive capacities go to the saint to get help and find solutions. One of the important functions of sanctuaries is precisely their involvement with sexuality and fertility. Indeed, if power can be defined as 'the chance of a person or a number of persons to realize their own will in a communal action, even against the resistance of others who are participating in the action,'[9] then women's collaboration with saints is definitely a power operation. Excluded from ritualistic orthodox religion, women walking in processions around saints' tombs express their quest for power in the vast horizons of the sacred space, untouched, unspoiled by human authority and its hierarchies:

> Pale young girls throw red flowers into the spring, others sugar or honeycombs, so that their voices may become sweet, spiritual, persuasive. The women who throw musk dream of being loved. . . . None goes to the spring without henna, without benjamin. While burning her green or red candle, the virgin says, 'Master of the spring, light my candle' which means 'marry me', or else 'give me splendid health.' The power to which they speak is capable of granting them all the goods of the world: life, strength, fortune, love, children. [10]

Now this quest for power that underlies the woman–saint relation is further confirmed by the fact that there are women saints who occupy a pre-eminent place and who specialize in solving problems of sexuality and reproduction.[11] They assume what Freud would certainly have called a phallic role and function. Some female saints go beyond the stage of penis envy and reverse traditional patriarchal relations: they are the ones who give penises to men suffering from sexual disturbances; such is the case of the Algerian female saint, Lalla Nfissa.[12] But this is not their only function. Unlike the emphasized passivity of women in the material, real worlds, supernatural women lead intensively active lives, perform all kinds of acts, from benign motherly protection to straightforward aggression, such as rape of men.[13] These women in the supernatural realm do not respect the traditional Muslim sexual division of labour which excludes women from power in religion and politics. In the supernatural realm, women may refuse to assume domestic roles, and play active roles in both religion and politics.

In one of the most respected biographies of the saints, the 13th-century *Al-Tasawwuf ila rijal al-tasawwuf*,[14] the biographer, Abu Yaqub al-Tadili, makes no specific reference to the fact that some saints were women: they enjoyed exactly the same rights and privileges and assumed the same characteristics as male saints. At one point, a woman saint, Munia Bint Maymoun Al-Dukali, says, 'This year, hundreds of women saints visited this sanctuary.' At another, a male insists that, 'In Al-Masamida [a region], there were twenty-seven saints who have the power to fly in the air, among whom fourteen are women.'[15]

Female saints seem to fall into two categories, those who are saints because they were the sisters, wives, or daughters of a saint[16] and those who were saints in their own right.[17] Many of these saints have strikingly 'unfeminine' personalities and interests. Imma Tiffelent, for example, literally fled her domestic condition:

> Not wanting to marry, Imma Tiffelant took the shape of a dove, escaped, and became a prostitute. . . . Twenty-seven young men disappeared after having loved her. Then she became an ascetic, in a hut, at the top of the mountain. . . . Ragged, unkempt, she preached religion in the valley, returned to her hut, shed even her rags, lived nude, and prophesied. It is forbidden to touch the trees around her grave, to kill the birds, to take the partridge eggs from the nest. [18]

The same identical flight from patriarchal 'womanhood' can be seen in Sida Zohra El Kouch, 'who was as wise as she was beautiful, resisted Moulay Zidane, died a virgin, and receives visits only from women.'[19] No less important, a prolific body of literature shows that a number of female saints played important roles in the political arena.[20] One of the most famous is certainly the Berber saint Lalla Tagurrami, who played a strategic role in her region's history as a referee in conflicts between tribes and between tribes and the central authority.[21] Politically, she was so influential and successful that the king imprisoned her:

> As she was among the most beautiful girls of the village, she was
> sought after for marriage, but refused all suitors. . . . Her reputation
> as a saint grew and extended far. The sultan wanted to meet Lalla
> Aziza and asked her to come to Marrakesh. Once there, she continued
> to distinguish herself by her piety and the good she did. She was
> greatly honoured, but her influence became so great that the sultan
> took offence and had Lalla Aziza thrown into prison. She was
> poisoned and died.[22]

It is of course possible that her fate was devised by myth tellers to
discourage other women from taking such paths.

Male Saints as Anti-heroes

Male saints, on the other hand, were profoundly concerned with what
we would call a housework issue: how to eat without exploiting
somebody else's work. Most analyses of lives of the saints fail to
emphasize their constant preoccupation with food and its preparation;
that they walk on water and fly in the skies is given more weight than
their efforts not to exploit the traditional domestic labour force available
– women. Around this question clustered all other issues, such as the
repudiation of possessions, privileges, political power, and the
condemnation of wars and violence, the very characteristics of a
phallocratic system. Most saints fled urban centres and their
sophisticated exploitative lives, tried hunting, fishing, gathering, and
cooking for themselves. [23] Some fasted as often as they could[24] and
trained themselves to eat very little; one went as far as to feed himself
on one mouthful.[25] Still others had supernatural help which ground their
own wheat or simply which gave them food.[26] They all tried to do
without housework and to avoid food cooked by others,[27] and they also
tried, to the community's dismay, to perform daily domestic chores
themselves, such as taking the bread to the neighbourhood oven.[28] One
of the most famous of saints, Bou Yazza, went so far as to assume the
appearance of a female domestic and to serve a woman for months.[29]

Some saints had families and children, some abstained and lived in
celibacy. But those who married were unsuccessful fathers and husbands
and lived like embarrassed heads of families who can't provide properly
for their dependents.[30] Others, especially elderly saints, did not hesitate
to renounce their marital rights when these appeared to be totally

opposed to the woman's happiness.[31] They definitely did not play the patriarchal role well. Among those who did not marry, one saint explained he was afraid of being unjust to his wife;[32] apparently, he saw marriage as an unjust institution for women. Another said he saw a beautiful woman walking down the street and thought he was in Paradise; she was exactly like a houri, one of the females provided to good Muslim believers in Paradise.[33] Although he secluded himself because he was afraid females would turn him away from God,[34] he did not identify them with the devil, as classical Muslim ideology does, but with Paradise, the most positive aspect of Muslim cosmogony.[35] Another saint fainted when he found himself alone with a woman in a room,[36] an unmasculine gesture to say the very least. Such fears are not those of a self-confident, patriarchal male.

Like the women who come to visit their sanctuaries, a large number of saints were of humble origin and were involved in manual or physical activities working as shepherds, butchers, or doughnut makers.[37] Others had no jobs and lived off nature, eating wild fruits, roots, or fish. Some saints were learned men, e.g. judges, who refused to use their knowledge to obtain influential positions and accumulate wealth, or even to teach,[38] and encouraged illiterates to be proud of their illiteracy. Like the women in the sanctuaries, however, many of them were illiterate. They reminded their communities, who respected them, of their illiteracy,[39] perhaps in order to demystify knowledge as a prerequisite for decision-making positions. Moulay Bou Azza made a point of not speaking literate or even colloquial Arabic.[40] Moulay Abdallah Ou Said, for example, tried to practise a teaching method for the masses 'without the intervention of written texts.'[41] Although shocking the learned mandarins, the illiterate female saint Lalla Mimouna constantly insisted she did not use the customary complicated Qur'anic verses in her prayers because she did not know them. 'Mimouna knows God and God knows Mimouna'[42] was the prayer she invented. This resistance to hierarchical knowledge is a persistent characteristic of saints' lives and their battles, which finds sympathy with the oppressed of the new developing economies: the illiterates, who are predominantly women. It is, therefore, no wonder that in the disintegrating agrarian economies of the Maghreb, sanctuaries, among all institutions, are almost the only ones visited spontaneously by women and where they feel at home. The sanctuary offers a world where illiteracy is not a hinderance to being a wholesome, thinking, and reasonable person.

* * *

The psychic and emotional value of women's experience in sanctuaries is uncontested and evident. Sanctuaries, which are the locus of anti-establishment, anti-patriarchal mythical figures, provide women with a space where complaint and verbal vituperations against the system's injustices are allowed and encouraged. They give women the opportunity to develop critical views of their condition, to identify problems and try to find their solution. At the same time, women invest all of their efforts and energies in trying to get a supernatural force to influence the oppressive structure on their behalf. This does not affect the formal power structure, the outside world. It has a collective therapeutic effect on the individual women visitors, but it does not enable them to carry their solidarity outside, to affect the system and shape it to suit their own needs. For these needs spring from their structural economic reliance on males and on the services they must give in exchange: sex and reproduction. The saint in the sanctuary plays the role of the psychiatrist in the capitalist society, channelling discontent into the therapeutic processes and thus depriving it of its potential to combat the formal power structure. Saints, then, help women adjust to the oppression of the system. The waves of resentment die at the sanctuary's threshold. Nothing leaves with the woman except her belief that her contact with the saint triggered mechanisms which are going to affect the world, change it, and make it suit her conditions better. In this sense, sanctuaries are 'happenings' where women's collective energies and combative forces are invested in alienating institutions which strive to absorb them, lower their explosive effect, neutralize them. Paradoxically, the arena where popular demonstrations against oppression, injustice, and inequality are most alive become, in developing economies, the best ally of unresponsive national bureaucracies. Encouragement of traditional saints' rituals by administrative authorities who oppose any trade unionist or political movement is a well-known tactic in Third World politics.

Notes

1. Gathering of historical data on saints, mainly female saints, was done with the collaboration and under the critical supervision of the Moroccan historian, Halima Ferhat, a Maître de Conférence at the University Mohammed V.

2. Then, in 1977, about 50p.

3. Emile Derminghem, 'Les Edifices', in *Le Culte des saints dans l'Islam maghrébin* (Paris: Gallimard, 1954), p. 113.

4. *Ibid.*

5. Mary Douglas, *Natural Symbols: Exploration in Cosmology* (New York: Random House, Vintage Books, 1973), p. 36.

6. *Recensement général de la population et de l'habitat*, 1971 (Rabat: Direction de la statistique, Ministère de Planification, 1971), 3:5. The illiteracy is estimated at 75

per cent for rural women between the ages of ten and twenty-four and between 93 per cent and 97 per cent for older women.

7.   Mircea Eliade, *Le Sacré et le profane* (Paris: Gallimard, 1965), p. 27.

8.   Fatima Mernissi, *Beyond the Veil* (Cambridge, Mass.: Schenkman Publishing Co., 1975), esp. the chapter entitled 'The Traditional Muslim View of Women and Their Place in the Social Order'.

9.   Max Weber, *From Max Weber, Essays in Sociology*, trans. and ed. with an introduction by H. Gerth and C. Wright Mills (New York: Oxford University Press, 1958), p. 180.

10.   Desparmet, 'Le Mal magique', in Derminghem, p. 44.

11.   Léon L'African, *Description de l'Afrique*, trans. from Italian by E. Epaulard Adrien (Paris: Maison Neuve, 1956), p. 216; and E. Doutté, *Magie et religion dans l'Afrique du Nord* (Alger: Typographia Adolphe Jourdan, 1908), p. 31.

12.   Derminghem, p. 43.

13.   Vincent Crapanzano, 'The transformation of the Eumenides: A Moroccan example' (unpublished manuscript, Princeton University, 1974), and 'Saints, jinns and dreams: an essay on Moroccan ethnopsychology' (unpublished manuscript, Princeton University, Department of Anthropology).

14.   Abu Yaqub Yusuf Ibn Yahya Al-Tadili, *Al-Tasawwuf, vie de saints du sud Morocain des V, VI, VIIIème siècles de l'Hégire. Contribution à l'étude de l'histoire religieuse du Maroc*, ed. A. Fauré (Rabat: Editions Techniques Nord Africaines, 1958). I will refer to this work as *Tasawwuf* and cite the number of each saint's biography.

15.   *Tasawwuf*, no. 160, p. 312; no. 209, p. 397.

16.   See *Tasawwuf*, no. 250, p. 431; no. 7, p. 70; no. 25, p. 111; and Derminghem, Lalla Mimouna, p. 68; Lalla A'isha, p. 125; Mana A'isha, p. 107.

17.   See *Tasawwuf*, no. 160, p. 312; no. 209, p. 397; no. 207, p. 397; no. 207, p. 394; no. 210, p. 398; no. 167, p. 331.

18.   Trumelet, 'Blida', and 'Saints de l'Islam', as quoted in Derminghem, p. 53.

19.   Derminghem, p. 49.

20.   Jacques Berque, *Structures sociales du Haut Atlas* (Paris: Presses Universitaires de France, 1955). p. 296.

21.   *Ibid.*, pp. 281, 286.

22.   *Ibid.*, p. 290.

23.   *Tasawwuuf*, no. 73, p. 186; no. 67, p. 170; no. 13, p. 88; no. 87, p. 217; no. 12, p. 86; no. 59, p. 162.

24.   *Tasawwuf*, no. 68, p. 76; no. 96, p. 228; no. 33, p. 124.

25.   *Tasawwuf*, no. 25, p. 111.

26.   *Tasawwuf*, no. 93, p. 223; no. 63, p. 171; no. 54, p. 156.

27.   *Tasawwuf*, no. 62, p. 166; no. 132, p. 184.

28.   *Tasawwuf*, no. 93, p. 224; no. 77, p. 197; no. 162, p. 321.

29.   *Tasawwuf*, no. 77, p. 200.

30.   *Tasawwuf*, no. 92, p. 222; no. 51, p. 152; no. 48, p. 144; no. 34, pp. 125-26.

31.   *Tasawwuf*, no. 99, p. 233; no. 56, p. 158.

32.   *Tasawwuf*, no. 45, p. 141.

33.   Qur'an, Sura 44, verses 53-54.

34.   *Tasawwuf*, no. 84, p. 214.

35.   Abu Hasan Muslim, *Al-jam'a al-Sahih* (Beirut: Al-Maktaba al-Tijaria, n.d.).

36.   *Tasawwuf*, no. 94, p. 224.

37.   *Tasawwuf*, no. 10, p. 79; no. 26, p. 115; no. 96, p. 228.

38.   *Tasawwuf*, no. 17, p. 95; no. 69, p. 178; no. 6, p. 69.

39.   *Tasawwuf*, no. 93, p. 223; no. 77, p. 197.

40.   V. Loulignac, *Un Saint Berbère – Moulay Bou Azza; Histoire et légende* (Rabat: Hesperis, 1946), 31:29.

41.   Jean Chaumel, *Histoire d'une tribu maraboutique de l'Anti-Atlas, le Aît Abdallah ou Said*, vol. 39, 1er et 2ème trimestre (Rabat: Hesperes, 1952), p. 206.

42.   Cited in Derminghem, p. 69.

CHAPTER V

Virginity and Patriarchy

It is no secret that when some marriages are consummated, the virginity of the bride is artificial. Enough young women to delight the gynaecologists with the relevant skills, resort to a minor operation on the eve of their wedding in order to erase the traces of pre-marital experience. Before embarking on the traditional ceremonies of virginal modesty and patriarchal innocence, the young woman has to get a sympathetic doctor to wreak a magical transformation, turning her within a few minutes into one of Mediterranean man's most treasured commodities: the virgin, with hymen intact, sealing a vagina which no man has touched.

Curiously, then, virginity is a matter between men, in which women merely play the role of silent intermediaries. Like honour, virginity is the manifestation of a purely male preoccupation in societies where inequality, scarcity, and the degrading subjection of some people to others deprive the community as a whole of the only true human strength: self-confidence. The concepts of honour and virginity locate the prestige of a man between the legs of a woman. It is not by subjugating nature or by conquering mountains and rivers that a man secures his status, but by controlling the movements of women related to him by blood or by marriage, and by forbidding them any contact with male strangers.

The Link between Women and Nature

It is not really surprising that the men of Mediterranean countries, where this phenomenon is particularly strong, should continue to use an outdated and stagnant technology, especially in agriculture. It is as though there were a haemorrhage somewhere preventing these peoples, who are cultured and sophisticated in other respects, from controlling the only entity which might measure up to them in a society which worships virginity: nature, the seat of survival. For the Mediterranean culture is one in which the subordination of men to capricious and unpredictable natural forces is equalled only by the subordination of women to men, as though there were a strange link, albeit a veiled and distorted one, between women and nature, both being uncontrollable except by reversing the natural order of things. And that is in fact the aim of the institution of virginity: to prevent women from producing children according to the rhythms of biology, the rhythms of pleasure, the rhythms of desire. It is not surprising that Catholicism, the religion which is *par excellence* opposed to pleasure, and which defines the sexual act as sinful if it is not for procreation, has made virginity into a deity. This one example shows how wrong it would be to underestimate virginity as a symptom of deeply and painfully buried conflicts, as a bearer of messages of which the importance has nothing to do with the insignificant bit of hymen which represents them. Other cultures have chosen different parts of the body to symbolize conflict and distress, the feet or the neck in some places, the cheeks or the foreskin in others.

But what is now new is that virginity is sometimes artificial: cracks and flaws have thus undermined the foundations of the *status quo* between the sexes. At the same time, however, women have realized that in order to insulate men from shock, in order to preserve their illusions, to avoid confronting them with a reality which they find so disturbing, it remains necessary to keep up appearances. The cost is high – between 500 and 1000DH (the average annual expenditure of a family of agricultural workers is 65DH, which immediately indicates the social classes in which these games are played). But the price is lower than before: it was 2000DH in 1968, which proves that this operation[1] is more common than it was a few years ago.[2] But the real question is as follows: why should a woman play such a crude trick on the man with whom she will spend her life and with whom she will, for decades to come, share her children, joys, sorrows and secrets? Is this not a real betrayal of the man who has chosen her?

The Lack of Understanding Between the Sexes

In fact, this strange practice, so typical of 'modernization' in which the artifices of the most up-to-date medical technology are placed at the service of the age-old imperatives of the patriarchal family, is the embodiment of the lack of understanding which for centuries has characterized the relations between the sexes. This lack of understanding is the result of inequality, an inequality which continues to flourish wherever economic lethargy prevails, and where the erosion of customs and traditions is all the deeper and the more insidious for being unrecognized or denied. The most tragic condition, as we approach the year 2000, is that of individuals and groups who live passively through changes while refusing to admit that they have happened, and who are thus quite unprepared to make new choices in order to preserve the only values which deserve to be preserved: dignity, and respect for oneself and for others.

Artificial virginity is degrading not only for the woman who buys it, but also for the man who penetrates her and for the couple which is created, a couple locked for ever in deception.

One of the manifestations of the lack of understanding between the sexes is that the sexual act is considered to be the sole responsibility of the woman. Defloration, like pregnancy, is, contrary to what is sometimes thought, an act which requires two agents: a man and a woman. Although patriarchal morality places the responsibility for defloration upon the woman, the law on the subject is very clear. Legally, any sexual act between two people of different sexes who are not united by the bond of marriage is a crime, and both partners are liable to the same term of imprisonment from one month to one year (Article 490 of the Penal Code). This contrast between the logic of the law, which establishes the responsibility of both partners for the sexual act, and the irrationality of the masculine mentality, which selfishly pushes the responsibility for defloration onto the woman alone, would be enough to explain the equally illogical and selfish response of women who resort to the trickery of false virginity.

From another point of view, artificial virginity exists because men ask the impossible: they want access to women for brief sexual encounters before marriage, but once they have decided to marry, they launch into a frantic search for a virgin whom no other man has 'defiled'. Such a man stands a good chance of penetrating crass stitches put in by a clever gynaecologist, and this is in fact a just turn of events because he too has 'defiled' the other young women before marriage; sex is defilement, sexual contact is a degrading experience which degrades the woman and, by the same token, any men who are linked to her by ties of blood or marriage. And he, the hero, destroys the honour of all these men by means of their young women, and will, on his wedding day, win the greatest victory of all by marrying that rare jewel, a woman whom no man has ever touched.

If men really respect virginity, they should be honest with themselves: they should refrain from having sexual contacts outside marriage, and refrain from pre-marital sexual relations. To suggest this in an Arab context makes one smile, yet it is precisely this which revolutionary leaders ask of their young people. They advocate abstinence and patience for both sexes, and the cold severity of the revolution is imposed with equal harshness on young men and young women alike. It is true that there is a great difference between Chinese leaders and Arab leaders.

The Great Tragedy of the Patriarchal Male

Sexuality is one of the most malleable of human characteristics, and societies have always made use of this fact in order to harness it to their ends, sometimes at the cost of enormous damage. To see this, one only has to look at classical anthropological texts, and at anthropological literature on the so-called developed countries, particularly that describing sexual behaviour in the suburbs of Paris and New York, the result of capitalism geared to the consumption of useless commodities.[3]

In any case, the picture of a male virgin trembling with purity and innocence on the eve of his wedding is, for the Arab man, the height of absurdity. This, however, is what he wishes to impose on the Arab woman. That is the great tragedy of the patriarchal male: his status lies in irrational schizophrenic contradictions, and is vested in a being whom he has defined from the start as the enemy – woman and her subterranean silence, woman who engulfs him in a sea of lies and in swamps of sordid manipulation. The law of retaliation: an eye for an eye, a lie for a lie . . . . The vicious circle of an impossible dialogue between partners mutilated by an insane patriarchy.

In three articles on the psychology of love,[4] Freud shows us the motivation and the behaviour of the patriarchal unconscious. He reminds us firstly that the taboo of virginity is buried in the most primitive recesses of human memory, and that it is a manifestation of man's fear of woman, a fear arising in the first place from her crushing superiority – only she could create life in and through blood – and in the second place from his suspicion that woman, behind her veil of obedience, would be plotting her revenge. Patriarchy also sets up a total split between affection and sexuality: men make the wife they 'respect' frigid, and choose for their pleasure women of the 'lower orders', slaves yesterday, prostitutes today. The logical conclusion of this split is impotence, which Freud identifies as a psychological phenomenon: the man who cannot perform the sexual act with a partner who is 'ideal' according to his own standards, and whom he respects, and can only achieve it with a woman he buys or despises. Freud's articles lead us into the vagaries of the pathological, the twists of the tortured and torturing love of those who are unable to mutilate themselves sufficiently to become virile according to the demands of a system which fears woman's body and expends all its efforts on damaging it, on making it ugly, on hiding its beauty and its brilliant power.

Social Schizophrenia

Men transform themselves into dirt to pollute their partners, and by the same token they turn the sexual act into an act of destruction and degradation. The deflowered virgin becomes a lost woman, but the man, like the legendary phoenix, emerges from the fray purer, more virile, better respected. In psychopathological terms, this is known as schizophrenia: a contradiction so total, so all-embracing that neither individual men nor whole societies can accept it as valid without destroying themselves. For the patriarchal sexual act is childish, it is the act of a man who has never outgrown the terrible fear of his insignificance in relation to the life-giving mother, and who has never become adult enough to see sexual pleasure as a relation between equals rather than as a mechanism for establishing a hierarchy and enforcing power, domination and therefore dehumanization.

If men really respect virginity, all they have to do is to set it up as exemplary pre-marital conduct as important for men as it is for women. It seems very likely that these young men encounter genuine virgins on their wedding day – no need for surgery in a country like Papa Mao's China, where people were trained to discipline their instincts and to harness them to the ultimate goal: national development. The virginity which China still imposes on its men and women has an aim which is rational and perfectly well integrated into an overall plan for national resources; this aim is to reduce the number of births. Women are at their most fertile before the age of thirty. To ask men not to touch them before this age, and women not to marry until their thirties is the most draconian method of keeping the birth rate down. But in Arab countries, what economic need does virginity serve?

Of what national plan is virginity a part? Does it just float, artificial and venal, in the mire of a disordered morality, without any coherent direction of aim? Religion lays down that both sexes should be virgins at marriage, and this one fact reminds one how much Islam is flouted every day by men who claim to adhere to its principles. Respect for religious law would therefore require a fundamental change in men's mentality and personality, a complete re-evaluation of their relations with the opposite sex, and the acquisition of sound and consistent principles upon which to build their lives.

But at this point one must ask if virginity is a social concept, regulated only by custom and tradition, or whether it is a legal phenomenon, laid

down by law. In the *Code de Statut Personnel*, elaborated in what is referred
to as the Mudawana, virginity is mentioned in Article 42 with reference
to the administrative formalities prior to marriage: it is stated that the
marriage deed should contain 'all relevant information on the state of
the bride, virgin or woman.' In Article 27 of the same Code, it is stated
that the 'bridegroom cannot insist that the marriage be consummated
before he has paid the bride the portion of the *sadaq* (dowry) which is
owing to her.' The money, it is added, cannot be claimed if
consummation takes place before payment has been made. In the Penal
Code relating to 'crime and offences against family order and public
morality', virginity is mentioned indirectly with reference to rape which
is usually punishable by 5 – 10 years' imprisonment, but carries a penalty
of 10 – 20 years' imprisonment if the woman is a virgin. The penalties
laid down for indecent assault are also increased if defloration occurs
(Article 488). The Mudawana and the Penal Code are cautious about
the prerogatives of the husband of a woman not previously married if
she turns out not to be a virgin. But this caution on the part of the law
is amply compensated by the prevailing rituals and customs, particularly
the displaying of the underwear worn on the wedding night, a ritual
which points to the primarily social nature of virginity. It is reported that
in some areas a special *bid'a* (innovation) takes place: it is said to be
fashionable not only to display on a platter the underpants stained with
blood, but also to adorn them with a certificate of virginity duly obtained
from a doctor and attached to the garment with a safety pin to prevent
it from slipping. In any event, the dramas and scandals undergone by
the families of both bride and bridegroom, if there is any doubt about
the virginity of the bride, are well known; this explains why young
women resort to artificial hymens and a demeanour of innocence which
they adopt all the more fiercely in proportion to the jealousy and
suspicion of their fiancé; any attempt at openness would lead to a breach.
In order to dispel suspicion, the bride-to-be must therefore display
childish behaviour and a studied ignorance, and must look to her fiancé
to take the initiative. She must deny her own existence so that he can
make her exist. What greater spur to the pride of a man who fears a
relation of equals than a woman who offers him the greatest role of the
patriarchal ideal, that of master? But if women are so well aware of men's
wishes, why do they not make sure that they remain virgins? Why do
they give in to other men who probably care very little for them? Why
do they condemn themselves to a comedy as degrading for themselves
as for men? This is the question that men ask themselves.

The Consequences of Inequality

The explanation lies in the ideological roots of the traditional Muslim family, which condemns women alone to monogamy and the control of sexual instinct. Men, by contrast, accept no such limitations: they can have as many partners as they choose. As well as four legal wives, each man has the right to as many concubines as his purchasing power permits. Moreover, repudiation permits him to change his legal sexual partners as many times as he wishes. 'Depressing' economic realities have led men to forego an establishment still strongly rooted in the collective memory, the harem. The institution of concubinage has gradually disappeared following the prohibition in Morocco around the 1930s of the practice of enslaving women. But even though harsh reality has eroded men's right to unlimited promiscuity, the principle has remained inviolate; the Mudawana of 1957 confirms the right of the husband to polygamy and to repudiation. And wherever there is inequality, there is also dishonesty, subterfuge, hypocrisy, and a wish, whether acknowledged or not, for revenge. It is self-evident that in societies which give one sex but not the other the right to several partners, a more or less silent dynamic of strife must become evident and manifest itself in more or less aggressive forms of behaviour. The practice of magic is one of these: women try, by means of age-old rituals and signs, to win and retain the love of men when they have no strict right to it. This absence of right has far-reaching consequences: doctors, especially in the south, report cases of patients in emergency wards who claim that they have been poisoned by philtres administered by their wives. There is no shortage of rumours about cases such as these, from particularly highly valued hyenas' heads which the hunters have been requested to hand over to the authorities, to the sperm whale of Sehb Edhab (a location in Morocco).[5] However, it is not the truth of the rumours which is important here, but their symbolic value as indicators of fantasy, need, desire and tension. The arsenal of manipulations at the biosexual level points in the same direction: medical virginity is only a modern version of the old-fashioned chicken's blood which used to be sprinkled on the underpants of so-called virgins, not to mention the other devices which old women passed on from generation to generation, not to mention fake pregnancies, fake births, fake orgasms. Each time a woman is cornered between the satisfaction of her own needs and conformity with a contradictory set of demands imposed on her by her social group, she resorts to trickery, which is the corollary of inequality. If she is unmarried and wishes to be married, a woman will arrange a false or a real pregnancy in order to put pressure on a lover who is seeking to evade his 'responsibilities', as they say. If she is married and infertile, she will have no hesitation in leading her husband and everyone else to believe in the birth of her child, which in fact is the barter of the child of another woman who did not want it for social or economic reasons. As for faked orgasm, it is too common even to mention.

Social Changes and the Reorganization of Space

The phenomenon of artificial virginity is therefore not ideologically new, but it is sociologically new, and it leads to the following question: why are there more fake virgins than before? The changes which have taken place in Moroccan society make virginity – which is a social, not a natural concept, since the body of both sexes is designed to be sexually active almost from puberty – more and more problematic. It is possible to identify at least four completely different kinds of change which have created a context in which the preservation of virginity is no longer an automatic function of the social group, but instead an act of individual courage. These are spatial changes, institutional changes, economic changes and psychological changes, and they have overlapping and profound effects on everyday life.

The first category consists of institutional changes which comprise mainly a rearrangement of the space allotted to women, and, so to speak, sexual desegregation. This allocation of space completely overturns the ideal sexual dynamic which Muslim society had regulated with a host of meticulous details. In this schema, men and women did not have the same rights to the consumption of space: men moved around freely, women much less so, if at all. Previously, the presence of a woman outside the space of her home was an abnormal phenomenon mediated by a whole armoury of devices. The main such device was the veil, since it allowed women to move in men's space without being seen, and the main occasions were family ones (when relatives were present) or religious ones (visits to Marabouts, i.e. holy shrines). Thus, to this day, a woman standing in a street or sitting on a beach or in a café becomes the object of aggression and humiliation: the ageless collective memory which drives women back into domestic space breaks out violently. This ancient segregation of space was, moreover, enshrined in religious texts (Sura 22, verse 31, for example). In this sense the veil can be interpreted as a symbol revealing a collective fantasy of the Muslim community: to make women disappear, to eliminate them from communal life, to relegate them to an easily controllable terrain, the home, to prevent them moving about, and to highlight their illegal position on male territory by means of a mask. This is the logical conclusion of the almost phobic attitude of the community towards women. Hence the deep-seated and violent reactions to the rights which nationalists have defended and institutionalized for women in anti-colonial struggles. Hence, too, the importance of the action of Mohammad V, who publicly unveiled his daughter, the Princess A'isha, in Tangiers in 1947, and the impact of Allal al-Fasi who, in writing the text of the Arab Charter, insisted on women's right to education and to participation in social life, themes which are also to be found in his book *Al-Naqd al-thati*.

Changes in the law and in economic structures

These statements, so radical in the context of the traditional segregation of space, have been echoed in texts as basic as the Constitution of the country, of which Article 9 gives all citizens the right of free movement and the right to settle in any part of the kingdom. That this article is contradicted by other, less important legal texts does not detract from its progressive nature. It is an unequivocal declaration of the end of the segregation of women, who now, as citizens, have equal rights to education and work (Article 13). The very low rate of education amongst Moroccan women does not remove the revolutionary dimension of these rights, if revolution means 'a sudden and important change in the social and moral order, a complete transformation'. The constitution was putting an end to centuries of women's confinement, to centuries of rigid separation between the sexes. The reactionary ulema (learned men of religion) who were opposed to feminist tendencies in the Salafieh movement (a famous religious brotherhood with political influence) had good reason to take alarm: a new order was coming about. In mixed schools, at work, in the labour market, in offices, at conferences and in the course of various economic activities, the sexes were about to discover in each other dimensions different from the impoverished and limited sexuality of the patriarchal model. But one of the most effective means of controlling pre-marital sex was being destroyed, and the control of sexual activity was becoming practically impossible.

These changes were reinforced by the fact that, simultaneously, the economic structure of the family was undergoing violent transformations which entailed the demise of patriarchal power. Previously, the family was a self-sufficient unit of production whose function it was to mobilize the labour of the members of both sexes and to place them at the disposal of a patriarch who was both their employer and their provider. But nowadays the father is often unemployed: Hassan

Sebar estimates that unemployment stands at 35 per cent.[6] The bankruptcy of patriarchal authority is one of the repercussions of a state of affairs in which women and children are obliged to work.[7] One conclusion that can be drawn from this is that individualistic tendencies are growing stronger within the family, which has become a nuclear family [8] Apart from unemployment, another factor comes into play, namely emigration[9] which clearly illustrates the overthrow of the father, and which reduces his power to a mere formality at the same time as eroding the family unit.

The Pursuit of Adolescent Girls

For women and girls, the overthrow of the father entails the necessity of entering the labour market and bending to its laws. And these laws are harsh. Often, they compel a young woman of 17 or 18, a schoolteacher or a nurse or a typist, to live a long way from her parents; this separation casts these girls, brought up in the tight cocoon of the nuclear family, into a period of profound insecurity and loneliness. They find it necessary to form new ties with other people in the new places in which they work, and it is therefore natural that young women obliged to earn their own living find themselves, in the course of events, taking on the task of creating relationships with men of their own age which are completely different from traditional relationships. And this self-determination of women totally alters the relations between the sexes; it is no accident that advocates of revolution and of women's liberation have always emphasized the importance of integrating women into the tasks of building and developing the country.

But men oppose this integration. They hang on to their privileges and pursue these young women who are placed in an insecure position because their families cannot feed them. Moreover, they represent the only solution to all these girls' problems: marriage. In a country where fathers are unemployed and where women's education is poor, promotion by means of a man remains the only effective way of 'carving oneself a place in the sun'. Often, when men seduce young women[10] they play on all the advantages which are precisely what women are looking for: money and a secure job in the modern sector with all that that means in terms of prospects of comfort. The seduction of young women in Morocco by older men has a definite class basis. The most extreme case is the seduction of maids who are then abandoned to the tender mercies of maternity wards in the public health service.

Another example is the trail of executives in their forties and fifties sitting in their large cars (often company cars – a detail frequently forgotten) in front of girls' schools and colleges. And the worst of it is that it is young girls who are blamed for their weakness rather than the adult men who take advantage of unemployment and poverty in this way. Young girls will continue to allow themselves to be seduced as long as their economic future is blocked, darkened by an economy determined from outside. As to Mediterranean men, trained to seduce, pursue and dominate women, and incapable of conceiving of love as a total and profound exchange between two equals, they will continue to penetrate stitched hymens, as artificial as their relationships with women. Similarly, they will continue in their traumatized attitude towards change, and will remain attached to trivial social rules instead of controlling their environment, their space, the international market and its mechanisms, technology, energy, everything which ultimately shapes their lives.

The Symptom of Malaise

As long as men continue to see in the sexual act a schizophrenic transaction in which women are 'guilty' of acts in which men are necessarily involved, such as defloration, extra-marital pregnancy and prostitution, the relationship between the sexes will be based on lies and deceit. Artificial virginity, far from being a phenomenon of only secondary importance, is the symbol of an age-old malaise which has for centuries frustrated the desire of men and women to love and respect each other. It is a malaise which stems from sexual inequality, unnatural by definition, anti-social in its workings. A man who thinks he is 'defiling' his partners unconsciously thinks of himself as a source of pollution, not only sexually, but at all levels, and it is easy to imagine how little he will be capable of self-determination in, for instance, the sphere of politics. For the political and the sexual are closely linked: people's body image and self image are cards which the ruling classes have manipulated brilliantly throughout human history, which is unfortunately a history of exploitation. Seen in historical context, sexual relationships are a field which the class struggle appropriates and through which it expresses itself. In this context, one must examine the relations of production as well as the relations of reproduction, the problem of illiteracy amongst poor women, especially rural women, the problem of their exclusion from training and from the modern sector, as well as the link between all this and prostitution, which is becoming a real industry in countries where unemployment is high. It is therefore necessary to look at the problem of sexual services rendered by women of the lower strata as commodities in a patriarchal economic market dominated by the collusion of international imperialist forces and local compradores. Only in this way can one gain a true understanding of problems which are discussed in drawing rooms as moral or ethical phenomena unconnected with the social and economic structure of the country.

Notes

This chapter appeared originally as an article in *Lamalif*. No. 107, June/July 1979

1.   It is a matter of sewing up the torn hymen which remains even after repeated intercourse, and even after curettages and pregnancies. This operation, which consists of a simple row of stitches, of which the number depends upon the state of the hymen, is known as *hymenorraphie* or stitching of the remains of the hymen. When sutured, the hymen heals, and the woman miraculously becomes a virgin again.

2.   See *Lamalif*, No. 25. 'Le scandale de la virginité' by Nadia Bradley.

3.   An analysis of the manipulation of sexuality in capitalism which has become a classic in Reich's *Sexuality and Class Struggle*. Much more literary, but equally revealing, is the recent analysis of the American writer Kate Millett in her book *Sexual Politics*, published in 1970.

4.   'A special type of object choice made by men', 'The most prevalent form of degradation in erotic life' (1912) and 'The taboo of virginity' (1918) translated by Joan Riviere in *Sexuality and the Psychology of Love* (Collier Brook, 1963).

5.   See *Lamalif*, No. 105.

6.   'Planification et disparités sociales à travers quelques indicateurs', in *Libération*, March 9, 17, 1979.

7.   Fatima Mernissi, 'Changes in the contemporary Moroccan family, waning of the power of the father and emergence of the state as alternative', published in Arabic in *Revue de la Faculté des Lettres*, Nos. 2 and 3, Rabat.

8.   A. Radi, 'Adaptation de la famille au changement social dans le Maroc urbain', *BESM*, No. 135.

9.   See the same issue of *BESM*.

10.   Woman's body in endogenous society. Ph.D. thesis by Khalil Lamrani, Morocco, 1976.

CHAPTER VI

Population Planning Without Democracy? The Conflict between the Muslim State and Women

Thoughts on the Morocco Demographic and Health Survey

I
The Unbridled Sexuality of Women as Cause of the Population Explosion

A new medina-theory

Since the gradual closure of EC borders to immigrants from the Maghreb has again raised the problem of youth unemployment with some urgency, one can go scarcely anywhere without hearing disagreeable remarks about women who can't stop 'breeding'. Moreover, the statistics exist to set a scientific stamp on this spontaneous medina-theory (so called because of its analogy with the term 'media-telegraph' – a kind of rumour which, in countries where information is strictly controlled, takes on an extraordinary tone), should that be needed. People with nothing whatever in common – high-ranking officials in the Ministry of Health and taxi drivers, for example – never tire of telling us that women's fertility is undermining the balance of the economy. Daily, in Rabat, we see angry drivers shouting at some young woman in a *jellaba*, who is struggling along with two children in tow and another on her back: '*Qbet wladek!*' ('Look out for your kids!') It impossible to spend more than fifteen minutes with a high-ranking official without at some point hearing him moan: 'We'll never achieve anything with this runaway birth rate! If only our women were like Europeans, with no more than two children or even just one, we'd do great things'. Momentarily relieved, the official normally readjusts his tie, which affords him the chance to regain his credibility. The responsibility for the economic disaster is now placed firmly where it belongs: on the shoulders of the uncontrollable woman/uterus/floodgate.

Once again, women are the source of all problems. They it is who thwart the projects conceived and constructed by a wonderfully caring state. Arab women, particularly those who have curiously taken it upon themselves to remain illiterate (you get the impression listening to these sorts of ideas that women do everything within their power, despite the efforts of the ministries concerned, to stay illiterate), are the source and cause of all obstacles to development. Inadequate health and educational facilities are all, like unemployment, stealthily engineered by women.

At first sight, the statistical data prepared by high-ranking experts in this field from the Planning Ministry – a group with a very high masculinity rate – presents women's role as a very dubious one. 'The crude birth rate, which was 46.1 per thousand in 1962, put Morocco among the countries with a very high rate of births. At the 1982 census, that rate had fallen by some 9 points to reach 37 per thousand inhabitants', as the experts of the Statistical Office disconsolately observe.[1]

Naturally, the linking of the terms 'birth rate' and 'crude' does nothing for the image of women since it is known that, although it takes two to conceive a baby, women are the only ones to retain any mark of the marvellous moments of nocturnal intimacy and produce babies nine months later. The crude birth rate thus reveals in all its glory this power to produce human beings unbidden, while the statistics of the Ministry of Health and Planning present the fall in infant mortality, which went down in the interim from 18.7 per cent in 1962 to 12.5 per cent in 1982, as a triumph of culture over nature.

This marks a stunning success for the Health Ministry, since enormous efforts were actually put into that area. So, the documents tell us, Morocco's rate of natural population growth rose from 27.4 per cent in 1962 to 27.7 per cent in 1982, which means that based on these figures, for every thousand inhabitants, the population rises each year by 27.7 persons.[2] No, you have not misread this. What it means is that, despite all the efforts the Health Ministry puts into the health of mothers and children and into planning – and, in the Moroccan case, those efforts are enormous – the rate of natural population growth, which is the difference between the crude birth rate and the crude death rate, has not fallen. 'As a result of this parallel fall in the birth and death rates, the rate of natural growth of the Moroccan population has not undergone any variation. In other words, the population has continued to grow at the same rate'.[3]

Another point which makes women's guilt in this affair more than probable is that they seem to resist all the state's efforts to get them to adopt contraceptive methods. Whereas the rate of usage of contraceptives is 83 per cent in the UK, 79 per cent in France, 78 per per cent in Canada and 68 per cent in the USA, Moroccan women continue, with their Arab sisters, to put regional demographies out of kilter by 'refusing' to use contraceptives. The rate of usage in Morocco is no higher than 27 per cent and Algeria stands out with a spectacularly low rate of 7 per cent .[4] It is Yemen, however, which really takes the biscuit here with a rate of 1 per cent . Those who wish to blame Arab women for the failure of planning can find 'scientific' arguments for their case in figures of this kind.

Let us return, however, to Moroccan women. Why, in spite of the efforts deployed by the state, is the rate of population growth not falling? After all, the number of children per woman has fallen, partly thanks to vigorous family planning programmes: '... in the early 1960s, the average number of children per woman was about 7, with no noticeable differences between urban and rural populations. Twenty years later, in the 1980s, this average stood at 5.5 children per woman'.[5] The other side of the equation, of course, is the fact that all those innocent little girls of the sixties, born in the euphoria of independence, have now grown up into mothers clearly determined to thwart ministerial plans for economic recovery. Whatever the plans of the various ministries, and despite the falling overall fertility rate (the ratio of the annual number of births to the number of women of childbearing age, i.e. women between 15 and 49), more children are being born, simply because there are more mothers. This is the real extent of the fedmale plot against the state and its functionaries.

This natural rate of growth, i.e. the difference between the number of births and the number of deaths – the number of those who, like you and I, have had the fortune to survive and stay the course – make up that population for whose happiness, or at least whose well-being, the state is supposed to plan. It is this figure, then, which makes it possible to calculate how much sugar is needed for our tea, how much wheat for our (oh, so delicious) bread and, most importantly, how many houses, schools, buses and trains etc. we need. With this, one begins to see why all administrative ire is directed against the fairer sex.

II
The Notion of Ante-natal Care as a Revolution in the Relations between Women and the Muslim State
Female reproduction and male administrative efficiency

Normally, the efficiency of an agency charged with carrying out a programme is evaluated by comparing the results obtained with the objectives laid down at the outset, while taking into account, as a matter of course, the cost of the operation. One may then gain an idea of the cost by dividing the programme's budgets by the number of beneficiaries. The efficiency of the agency carrying out the programme would be higher and the costs lower where a large number of people benefited by it. Now according to the ante-natal care survey, only a third of the potential beneficiaries have been affected by its programmes. But, let us look more closely at this idea of the efficiency of services, an idea rarely mentioned in connection with services for women, as though there were no requirement on the public services to be efficient where they are concerned.

If one examines the programmes administered by the state, particularly where the potential beneficiaries are women, one soon arrives at the conclusion that, in most Arab countries, they are quite ineffective. With regard to the management of those health programmes aimed at providing ante-natal care for mothers and at helping them through pregnancy and labour, the proper way to proceed would be to divide the budget allocated by the number of beneficiaries. Now, we are living in Arab countries where the first rule of the system is secrecy in financial matters. The absence of openness where financial dealings and budgetary allocations are concerned is one of the structural characteristics of social (and other) programmes. In the health statistics, for example, the number of beneficiaries per province is given, but there is never any indication of the amounts expended that would enable us to assess the efficiency of the operation. In the absence of such budgetary openness, all we can do is evaluate the numbers of beneficiaries of these programmes. That evaluation is, in itself, quite revealing.

The concept of ante-natal care as a revolutionary notion in the societies of the harem and the *hijab* (veil)

The notion of ante-natal care is new and represents a definite break in the relationship between women and the state in societies where the *hijab* (veil) remains a fundamental concept. The concepts harem and *hijab* are inseparable and together ordain a division of labour between the state and the head of the family. In a Muslim society, the harem is the domestic space which is under the authority of the head of the family; he has sole proprietary rights over the bodies of the women there, together with monopoly control of their sexuality and reproduction. A rigidly defined code of honour gives him this monopoly and, in traditional society, violence against a woman who infringed the law of honour was not in any way punished by the state. There are occasional reports of crimes of honour in the Arab press, though it is always somewhat surprising to see them, since, as in the famous case of the Saudi Princess, considerable reserve is generally exercised in these matters. What is new is the surprise and embarrassment generated by the crime of honour, and this shows that Arab society is, nonetheless, undergoing change and transformation.

Within this context, the idea of a state – i.e. male civil servants in the main – concerning itself with women's pregnancy and labour represents a radical revolution. It is this radical revolution in mentalities and practices which the Arab world and Morocco are experiencing currently and this explains the confusions and impasses which have arisen. Debates on the veil, and fundamentalism with its persistent demand for the prohibition of coeducation are the product of these resistances and, by the very violence they arouse, enable us to see that, in spite of everything, deep transformations are taking place. One of the most important events this century is this redistribution of tasks between the state and fathers or husbands where the family and women's needs are concerned, and the official transference of the management of women's affairs, such as reproduction, and their education and employment, from the domestic to the public sphere. This certainly represents a profound revolution not only in sex roles, but also, most importantly, in the relationship between women and the state. In other words, it represents a total destructuring of the order of the *hijab*. With the emergence of women, at least at the level of state practices, as citizens and direct partners of the state – of a Muslim state which has never recognized any direct relationship with them – a genuine spatial revolution has taken place.

Without actually wishing to, the modern Arab state effects a fundamental revolution in mental schemas every time it interferes in the management of sexuality or fertility by way of family planning or mother-and-child health care programmes. But the Arab state does not adopt these programmes which are targeted at women as a result of an internal debate on its function or a process of philosophical and political reorientation. It adopts them – and this is the problem – under international pressure which takes the form of conventions (of the United Nations, for example) that have to be ratified if the state wishes to project a modern image, or to receive funding, where that funding is linked to population control. The history of the adoption of family planning in the Arab countries reveals that there has been – and still is – resistance to these programmes, which are in many cases financed in the first instance by foreign money. Underlying that resistance, which is often disguised by references to sacred texts, is a cultural fact: Arab women are considered the property of the head of the family, and the state does not regard itself as having any obligation to serve them. The concept of ante-natal care as defined by UNICEF, which is based on the observation that the rate of deaths in childbirth reveals one of the most glaring inequalities of this century of progress, is certainly a revolutionary concept in this connection:

> The most tragic of all these figures is the maternal mortality rate. All the social indicators (literacy, life expectancy or child mortality rates) reveal the enormous gap which separates the industrialized from the developing countries. . . . If we take all the various factors into account, the risk of dying of causes related to pregnancy and childbirth is at least 40 times higher in the developing world and, in some cases, even 150 times higher in the poorest countries. In Africa, we find almost 700 maternal deaths for every 100,000 live births. . . . In the industrialized nations, the average is less than ten. . . . It is possible to reduce the dangers of pregnancy and childbirth considerably by helping women to obey the following rules:
> • have regular check-ups during pregnancy,
> • ensure that a qualified person is present at the birth,
> • allow an interval of at least two years between births and avoid pregnancy before the age of 18. . . .[6]

This definition of care for mothers is a violation of the law of the harem (which comes from the root *haram* prohibition) and of the *hijab* (which comes from the root *hajaba* to conceal a space, to mark it off with a curtain or a symbolic boundary), which split society into two: those belonging to the domestic space and those belonging to the public space.

> The concept of *hijab* is three-dimensional and these three dimensions very often cut across each other. The first is a visual dimension: hiding from view. The root of the verb *hajaba* means to 'hide'. The second dimension is spatial: to separate, to mark a boundary, establish a threshold. Lastly, the third dimension is ethical: it relates to the

question of prohibition. At this level, we are dealing not with tangible categories which exist in the reality of the senses, such as the visual or the spatial, but with an abstract reality that is of the order of ideas. A space hidden by a *hijab* 'is a forbidden space'.[7]

The ante-natal care programmes of a Muslim state, where decision-making is monopolized by an almost 100 per cent male elite of civil servants, is a blatant intervention in the harem – the domain of women and their sexuality – on the part of men from outside the family. Ensuring access for women, and particularly poor women, to new services marks both a positive break with the mental categories which have excluded them from the public sphere and the emergence of women as modern citizens of a modern state working in the interests of all. The issue now to be addressed is how well the Moroccan state has carried this out. We must therefore turn to the outcome of these programmes of care for pregnant mothers.

The Results of the Morocco Demographic and Health Survey. More than two-thirds of Moroccan women give birth at home without a qualified person in attendance
The Morocco Demographic and Health Survey carried out in 1987 is an interesting study in that it relates to a sample of women from the most deprived sectors of the population. Almost half of these (47.6 per cent) live in accommodation with none or only one of the three indicators of minimum amenities (running water, private toilet, gas); almost two-thirds have neither refrigerator nor television (59.8 per cent). It might be said that these mother-and-baby health care programmes, which are among the rare ones the state provides for poor women, are to some extent exceptional, in that the state manifests its positive will towards economically marginalized women who tend in every way to be excluded.

However, the survey reveals that the impact of these programmes, the purpose of which is to provide care during pregnancy, labour and the first years of the child's life, is relatively disappointing, particularly in the light of the cost of such programmes in the Third World. A first result, which is rather surprising, is that two-thirds of women continue to give birth at home, as though the health infrastructure did not exist or applied only to a limited clientele. Only 26.3 per cent succeed in gaining admittance to a hospital to give birth. Of that number, only a third have the signal honour of being treated by a doctor. The others have to be content with the assistance of midwives and nurses during their labour.[8] This would not be so serious if those who had their children at home could catch up subsequently and receive the care the state is supposed to provide for them. Unfortunately, the survey reveals that there is a close link between the place of giving birth and the fact of benefiting from ante-natal or post-natal care. Of women giving birth at home, 82 per cent subsequently received no care, whereas 30 per cent of those who gave birth in a public hospital had access to such care. Of those who gave birth in the private sector, two-thirds received post-natal care.[9]

Generally, more than two-thirds of the sample (71.3 per cent of women) did not benefit from any ante-natal care. Of that third of women (28.7 per cent to be precise) who said they had received ante-natal care, almost half had received it through the private sector. Of a total sample of 3,753 women, only 555 – i.e. 14.7 per cent – had benefited from ante-natal care in public centres.[10] But access to a public hospital to receive ante-natal care in no way guarantees that one will be fortunate enough to be treated by a doctor. Only a quarter of these women were in fact seen by a doctor during their visits. The remaining three-quarters had to be content with the attentions of nurses and midwives.

Disappointing as these findings are, it is only in the light of certain correlations that we realize in fact the extent of the failure of these programmes. Factors like place of residence, poverty and age dramatically reduce the chances of benefiting from them. The fact of living in a rural area means virtual exclusion from these programmes. Only 10 per cent of women in rural areas bear children in hospital and almost 90 per cent of them give birth at home with all the obvious risks of complications, given the inadequacy of transport, particularly of ambulances. Only 14 per cent of rural mothers manage to obtain ante-natal or post-natal care. The fact of being poor virtually stigmatizes the mother. Only 5.7 per cent of those classed as living on the 'poverty threshold' give birth in hospital and only 7.9 per cent receive ante-natal care.

However, one of the most perplexing findings relates to the age of mothers. Paradoxically, the youngest of pregnant women, i.e. those with greatest need of ante-natal care, given the risks to first-time mothers, are in fact those who have least chance of receiving it. Mothers in the age-range 15–24, who are therefore the most vulnerable during their pregnancies, make up only 27.6 per cent of the women who have the good fortune to give birth in hospital. The remaining two thirds give birth at home, although the risks among that category are obvious [11]

What is surprising is that the National Statistical Bureau, which is probably the best-informed institution in Morocco since it specializes in providing us with facts and figures on social trends and developments, and which has distinguished itself in recent years by a remarkable – and widely praised – effort where information on reproduction and women in particular is concerned, in no way speaks of failure when it comes to the issue of health in its publication on women and the female condition in Morocco. Family planning is presented, in that 1989 document, as a success:

> Several operations have been conducted jointly to educate women in matters of nutrition, vaccination, access to contraceptive methods and care for expectant mothers. Thus between 1979 and 1985, the number of family planning centres has risen from 315 to 475. These centres carry out the distribution of contraceptives and provide related care. In 1986, the number of women using the pill, intra-uterine devices (IUDSs) or condoms for the first time had reached 432,170, whereas the 1979 figure was only 133,815. This represents a rise of 223 per cent.

Since the fall of the Berlin Wall, this kind of self-congratulatory utilization of statistics for purposes of rosy propaganda on television – or any of the other media the modern state has at its disposal – has quite simply become embarrassing, even in Third World countries. The emergence of openness as a key factor in efficiency was one of the lessons of the collapse of socialism in Eastern Europe. This lesson does not seem to have been learnt by Moroccan statisticians. They continue to trumpet the success of their programmes, even when they are in fact scandalous wastes both of energy and public funds. It is precisely this insensitivity of the state, and particularly of the technical services which have the job of describing, informing and evaluating the performances of the public services (especially those which have the life and death of high risk groups like pregnant women in their hands), which we now have to explain.

For what is scandalous is not so much the inefficiency of the public services in women's issues, but the fact that the failure is not even registered. For that failure to be registered, the public services would have to change so that they produced something other than systematic self-praise, beneath which one can in fact detect a sense of unease about the priorities and objectives of those services.

It might help us to enter the age of openness if expenditure figures were appended to the statistics on the performance of the state programmes (e.g. the number of pregnant women who have received care). If these programmes were to be judged by the number of people they reached, and if there were some evaluation of their ability to deliver care to the poorest and most deprived mothers – which is what justifies their existence – we would have to admit failure, or at least show some humility about the practical achievements. If the state were obliged to function in a climate of openness and on lines of efficiency, and if it had to question its own priorities when, relating the amounts invested to the number of beneficiaries, the real costs of those services were seen to be too high, we would have seen a real crisis within the Health Ministry once the results of this survey were known. But there was nothing of the sort. The fact that programmes directed at women do not attain their objectives is no kind of drama or tragedy for the state. It is quite simply a routine fact. And it is this absence of drama when the ineffectiveness is plain for all to see which we now have to analyse.

III
Why is the Ineffectiveness of the Public Services in Women's Issues not Perceived as a Scandal?
The notions of *qaid* and *hijab* as obstacles to citizenship

A matter which seems anodyne, not to say trivial, but which nonetheless merits close examination, is that key ministries like Health and Education, which deliver few services for women or deliver them very indifferently, are not regarded as scandalously inefficient institutions. Why is it considered normal in Arab countries, where state officials are forever on the television talking of the progress and the 'prodigious leaps forward' (*qafza hassima*) they are making, that the rates of female illiteracy and of exclusion of women from elementary health services remain among the highest in the world?

The conflict between citizenship and the notion of *qaid* (the destructive power of women), and the segregationist notion of *hijab*
The notion of *qaid* is a key one in the collective memory. Whenever a woman negotiates keenly over a contract or project and conducts her argument convincingly, sooner or later the famous verse 28 of Sura XII (Yusuf or Joseph) falls like an executioner's blade: '*inna kaydakunna la azim*' ('Verily, your devices are great!'). In fact the phrase recurs twice in this same verse, which gives it a prodigiously impressive effect, particularly as the passage in question establishes the guilt of a woman in an attempted adultery. *Qaid,* as *Lisan al-Arab* (one of the most authoritative Arab dictionaries) tells us, is '*al-khubth*' (wickedness

combined with meanness), '*al-makr*' (the coldly premeditated desire to destroy). Another synonym given to explain the notion of *qaid* is '*al-ihtiyal*', i.e. long-term and carefully conceived cunning.

In fact the component of premeditation, cold planning and calculated evil intent is essential in the notion of *qaid*: 'this is why', the dictionary tells us, 'war is called *qaid*'. In the Sura of Yusuf, *qaid* is a woman's decision to commit adultery. The *qaid* of women thus has to do with sexuality, with the possibility they always have of destroying order by offering themselves to men other than their husbands. Oddly, in this old medieval dictionary, the *Lisan*, Ibn Manzur tells us that if one says a woman is '*kaadat*', this means she is menstruating. But if this latter meaning has faded into the depths of memory, that of the subversive power of women to sow disorder through their sexuality, sensuality and powers of seduction is, by contrast, still very much alive and invoked daily.

The Sura of Yusuf, where we are told at the very outset, '*Nahnu naqussu alaika ahsan al-qassas*' ('In revealing to thee this Koran, one of the most beautiful narratives will we narrate to thee'), is certainly one of the most beautiful in the Qur'an. It tells, as is well known, of the first betrayal of Joseph by his brothers who throw him down a well. Being found by travellers, he is sold in Egypt to a chief, the Vizir, who adopts him as his son. One of the high points in this Sura is the moment when the Vizir's wife, who is not named in the Qur'an (except in relation to her husband, Imraat al-Aziz, the wife of the Vizir), disturbed by Joseph's beauty, sets about seducing him and has almost persuaded him to copulate with her when he changes his mind and manages to restore order. *Qaid* is, thus, this barely controllable power which emanates from women, and which they can mobilize, when they so decide, to destabilize the order of the fathers, the order of the masters. The way unemployment and the failures of the transport system are currently blamed on women and on the runaway birth rate, for which they are supposedly responsible, bring this notion to mind again and give it renewed importance today. It is indeed often referred to in conversation in variously leering tones when the subject in question is family planning.

Qaid is invoked almost daily in the streets of the medinas in the sense of practical cunning in everyday negotiations – haggling over the price of cloth or food – or in more serious and structured situations like ministerial meetings. When a woman makes a well-judged remark or negotiates subtly, cornering her opponent and forcing him to back down (over the price of goods or a clause in a contract), the phrase 'Verily, your devices are great!' is invariably heard.

This notion of *qaid* might also be seen as explaining the institution of *hijab*, where female sexuality is also regarded as a site of potential disorder and sedition. The *hijab* is a barrier which conceals women from the public space. As with *qaid*, the revelation of the verses on the *hijab*, such as verse 59 of Sura 33, where the Prophet's wives are advised to make themselves known by 'let[ting] their veils fall low' (*uyudnaina alayhinna min jalabibihinna*) — this is also linked to a sexual malpractice which occurred in Medina in the days of the Prophet. This was so-called '*ta'arrud*', men placing themselves in the way of women and harassing them with improper suggestions (*zina*). The only difference in this case is that the initiators of sexual disorder here are men and the *hijab* was institutionalized in order to protect women and put them in a forbidden, protected space.

This brief digression into Muslim memory is of interest in that it reveals to us that two major concepts in the Muslim psyche — *qaid* and *hijab* — both of which involve the misdeeds of a sexuality that is a source of disorder, are still very strong in the conscious life of modern Arabs, and in Arab political dynamics. The fact that fundamentalist movements, which are often in opposition to existing regimes, speak of co-education and women's access to public life as sources of disorder proves we are far from having made the necessary break that would take us into a society orientated by the conception of woman as citizen. Women's citizenship remains a goal still to be achieved, and its achievement will involve a process of education both of the masses and of the authorities.

Until we arrive at this conception of woman as an equal, responsible citizen, as neither a danger to be contained nor a subversive force to be hidden away and obliterated, but as a resource to be managed and a talent to be developed, every developmental project in the Arab world will be doomed to failure. We will be unable to make the transition from a society lost in fantasies and shot through with myths and archaic ideas to a scientifically orientated society which perceives human beings as resources and talents. And the education of women remains, in fact, one of the most certain means for making this transition; for women alone, by their daily participation in all fields of social life — especially in the most highly regarded such as politics — could make a palpable change here and set their country on a course which leads into the future. This is why education is such a key question and why we so need in the nineties to eliminate illiteracy, one of the most shameful blots on an Arab society that is so dynamic in other areas.

IV
Women's Education and their Participation in the Process of Democratization, particularly in Media Production, as Two Ways of Promoting the Wider use of Birth Control

There is currently in the Arab world an educated, qualified female élite, which is active in two key spheres of cultural activity: university research and the media. That élite already plays an important role, not only in terms of political opposition, but, most importantly, of cultural and media production. The films and books produced by women in the Arab world may not have changed the negative image of women cultivated by society, but they have at least created an awareness of the problem. Education is, therefore, a key factor in stimulating the rationalization of reproductive activity, since it has come to be seen as a determining factor in the lowering of the birth rate. However, though an élite of educated women has emerged, this remains an intrinsically urban phenomenon, and one limited particularly to the middle classes. The mass of poor women are still far removed from this happy condition.

There has been record investment in education in Arab countries, but this has been of little benefit to women. As yet, for the most part, the funding does not go to them. As we have just seen from the ante-natal care survey, almost two-thirds of mothers are excluded from that care. But that same survey reveals that an educated woman has three-and-a-half times more chance of receiving ante-natal care than an uneducated one. And, by the beginning of the eighties, all the studies carried out in Morocco, particularly the survey on contraceptive use, had already shown the direct link between education and family planning: 'The level of fertility falls with each rise in the level of education'. [12] Now, it is precisely this direct causal link between family planning and women's education which leads us to doubt the state's determination to plan rational development based on a scientific planning of resources, since this would have meant making the ending of women's illiteracy a priority. The fact is that, on this crucial question, the state does not seem particularly committed to effective action.

Despite its resources and dynamism, Morocco is among the Arab countries with the highest rates of female illiteracy. That rate is 78.3 per cent, and it is not much lower in Algeria (63.1 per cent). The figure for Egypt is 79.8 per cent and the former People's Republic of North Yemen had a rate of 74.8 per cent, whilst the figure for South Yemen was 96.6 per cent. The only Islamic country doing pioneering work in this field is Iraq with a rate of 12.5 per cent, with the result that it can be classified among those nations where women's access to education is 'administered normally'.[13] It is hardly surprising, then, to see international agencies accusing the Arab world of being one of the regions where women are kept in a state of ignorance, as for example in the comparative study produced by the Population Crisis Committee. In that study, ninety-nine countries were stringently evaluated with regard to the status of women and assessed in terms of twenty indicators designed to measure women's well-being. The study took in ninety-two per cent of the world's female population and produced a classification on the basis of indicators of health, education, employment and other social factors, particularly those relating to women's participation in the management of society.

As one might expect, the Arab states came at the lower end of the scale: 'Not surprisingly, North America and northern Europe dominated the top-ranked countries; Africa, the Middle East and South Asia, the bottom ranks. . . . The high-income, oil-exporting countries of the Gulf ranked very poor or extremely poor . . .'.[14] It is by contrasting these rates of female illiteracy with the rates for men that we understand the extent to which we are faced with a state that serves its citizens in a particularly discriminatory way. Since independence, Morocco has managed to provide schooling for something like half of its men (only 55.4 per cent are illiterate) and Algeria has succeeded in lowering its male illiteracy rate to 37 per cent. Tunisia has managed to educate two men in three (only 32.4 per cent are illiterate), but only 40 per cent of women have had access to that education. The revolutionary enthusiasm which fired the leaders of the now defunct People's Democratic Republic of Yemen did not prevent them from discriminating against women in educational matters. Two-thirds of men had access to education (only 41.1 per cent are illiterate), but the revolution only afforded that same level of instruction to one woman in four.[15] And yet the mass education of women was precisely what was needed if the Arab states really wanted to control their birth rates. The best partners in projects of this kind are educated women. Just a few years of schooling works miracles in this field. Indeed, the connection is so well established and the statistics so copious that it is surprising the nineties have not been declared a 'Decade for the abolition of female illiteracy' in Morocco and other Arab countries.

The whole future of family planning in the Arab world – and the Islamic world in general – does, in fact, depend on the education of women and their participation in the production of their own image by acquiring influence in the media. The incredible developments in telecommunications and the take-up of television by the masses indicate that it is to these technologies we should look to develop our future strategies.

Conclusion

There is every likelihood that rational family planning will become a mass practice among women once they begin to take an active part in other spheres of life and to gain a certain autonomy, a certain control over the management of their own lives and bodies. All the conditions for such a 'seizure of power' over their own lives and their environments are in place: an educated female élite, determined to change the image and status of women, and television, which has reached almost every middle-class home and is increasingly to be found in the homes of the poor. The Morocco Demographic and Health Survey has shown that even out of a sample in which 47.6 per cent have neither running water nor a private toilet, 18.5 per cent have both television and a refrigerator and 21.7 per cent have at least one of these. This massive penetration of television into the lives of even poor families reveals it to be a powerful means both for promoting the education of women and also for producing a more positive female image. Television will also surely be the best instrument for transforming the mentality of the Arab male. For all these reasons, we should devise strategies that would allow the female élite already working in the media to be able to play a greater role, particularly in the production of women's programmes, and films and videos in vernacular languages. We might even suppose that the development of a female media industry might be a way of promoting women in what is a key sector of the future. Training courses for women which would teach them to master the production of software designed for the education of millions of women could serve several purposes at once: bringing literacy to the most deprived, assigning a greater role to the female élite, and so democratizing the production of ideas and images in the Arab world.

This would be a very 'cool' and very peaceful way of setting democratization in train and forestalling the threat of a fundamentalism which only has so much influence because it overlaps with and reproduces the official discourse of the state. Giving women the chance to get other messages across and to make a contribution by formulating a different culture would already produce that 'plural' effect which is the essence of democracy.

It is illogical to expect a woman, whose will and initiative are hobbled in all other spheres by a society which perceives her as a source of *qaid*, a focus of negative forces, to develop an initiative in the field of fertility alone. The autonomy of a person is only conceivable if it is 'holistic'. The decline in the birth rate in the West is linked, among other things, to an increasing democratization of social relations and a greater

participation of women in the affairs of their communities. A democratization and a participation which took the form, in their individual
lives, of a more egalitarian access to education and employment. The
birth rate can be rationally managed, restricted or lowered, only as part
of a precise developmental project, if women are partners, or at least
included in one way or another, in that rationalization process. Nothing
is more irrational than the idea of inferiority or exclusion. Yet these
notions reflect the attitude of the Arab state towards women.

This is not an attitude exclusive to the Arab world, of course, but *the
Arab world is alone in not setting about the task of changing that inegalitarian vision*
by calling on women to participate at all levels. This is not a biological
problem but merely, in a sense, a technical one and it could be resolved
within a decade if a real media policy were put in place to that end and
funds were allocated for the purpose. To see the transformation in
mentalities after the Gulf War, the stirrings among the people during
that ordeal and the incredible solitude of the Arab leaders during this
interim period, one is rather optimistic about future prospects. For
everyone – including both the governors and the governed – has realized
that strength and prosperity lie in a rapprochement between the state
and its citizens, 50 per cent of whom are women. The passionate debates
around the veil and co-education and the wave of fundamentalism are
merely part of the inevitable turbulence involved in arriving at some
assessment of the situation, clarifying the problems, making the requisite
breaks, dissipating the ambiguities. And in this sense, fundamentalism,
together with the renewed debates on co-education and the veil, have
to be considered not as archaic regressions but as difficult processes of
transition to a modernity which requires violent breaks, the discarding
of old attitudes, and painful readjustments. And here the exploration of
the Muslim heritage, by way of films, books and feminist readings of
the past, remains one of the most rational and effective ways of standing
up to fundamentalism and shifting the focus on to the issues which really
count: the creation of equal opportunities in an environment which we
have to recognize as limited in its resources. The most promising future
strategies lie in the elucidation of the historical roots of concepts and
in looking to the Muslim heritage to develop audio-visual products or
books – including stories for young people etc. – which speak of
women's autonomy and identify it as an endogenous phenomenon. And
the point is not only that women in the Islamic world should achieve
the necessary autonomy to gain control over their own bodies, but also
that they should participate in a mode of living together on the planet
which involves learning a whole new way of perceiving life, death, the
planet, and the stars.

Notes

1. *Femmes et condition féminine au Maroc*, Royaume du Maroc, Premier Ministre, Direction de la Statistique, 1989, p. 24. The statistical terms used are defined as follows: crude birth rate (CBR) is the annual number of live births per 1,000 inhabitants; total fertility rate (TFR) is the number of annual births in relation to the total number of women of childbearing age (i.e. between 15 and 49); crude death rate (CDR) is the annual number of deaths per 1,000 inhabitants.

2. Ibid., p. 23.

3. Ibid., p. 24.

4. The figures for the rates of contraceptive use are taken from the UNICEF report *'La Situation des enfants dans le monde*, 1989, pp. 102-3.

5. *Femmes et condition féminine au Maroc*, p. 24.

6. *La Situation des enfants dans le monde*, p. 42.

7. F. Mernissi, *Le harem politique* (Paris: Albin Michel), p. 120.

8. *Morocco Demographic and Health Care Survey*, 1987, Table 3: Coverage of maternal health care.

9. Ibid., Table 4.

10. Ibid., Table 2.

11. Ibid., Table 5.

12. *Planification familiale, fécondité et santé familiale au Maroc (1983-1984): Rapport de l'enquête de prévalence contraceptive*, Ministère de la Santé Publique, Statistiques Sanitaires, February 1985, p. 59.

13. Abdelkader Sid-Ahmed, 'Le Monde Arabe Horizon 2000', UNESCO series 'Réflexion sur les problèmes mondiaux'. Workshop organized at ALESCO, Tunis, 12-14 September 1988. BEP/88/WS/33. Table 1, Estimate of illiteracy in the Arab states, p. 64.

14. Population Crisis Committee, 'Population briefing paper: country rankings of the status of women, poor, powerless and pregnant', June 1988, No. 20.

15. Abdelkader Sid-Ahmed, 'Le Monde Arabe Horizon 2000', op. cit.

Women's Work
Religious and Scientific Concepts as
Political Manipulation in Dependent Islam

It is not my purpose here to pursue an argument or to prove a hypothesis, as I did in my ILO study[1] on which this chapter is based. Here I would like to indulge in a plan considered rather dangerous in our Muslim societies: to question medieval religious concepts and selective Western scientific, economic, and statistical categories retained by our technocrats (legislators, planners, etc.) when dealing with women's work. Our medieval religious heritage is large enough to provide modern technocrats with all kinds of conceptual tools to trace and evaluate the changing patterns of women's contribution to modern Muslim economies, as is Western scientific, economic, and statistical accumulation of knowledge. Recent debates on better conceptual tools to evaluate housework and integrate it into national accounts, as well as debates on women's work in the informal sector and how to account for it in monetary terms (so as to give a more accurate view of the Gross National Product), are some of the issues which are particularly relevant to Third World economies.

With this wealth of sources from which to draw (i.e., centuries of Muslim heritage and centuries of Western industrialization in both capitalist and socialist economies) one wonders about the kind of conceptual tools that Muslim technocrats have devised since independence which underlie our understanding of the potential and utilization of human resources. How do these conceptual tools help us gain insights into one of the key processes of wealth creation: work in general, and women's work in particular? How close to reality are our national accounts when it comes to identifying and evaluating the multiple forms of women's contribution to the production of goods and services in Muslim economies?

The last question is particularly pertinent in Muslim societies where sexual segregation is still upheld as an ideal model of space management and where, therefore, woman's seclusion and confinement to domestic space is still considered by many as the 'natural' and right place for her. Any attempt to analyse women's work inside or outside the family, in the formal or informal sector, or in a paid or unpaid capacity cannot yield any pertinent results if sexual segregation is not taken into account.[2] The sexual segregation of space seems to encompass a whole range of sex roles and models which cannot be ignored if we are to understand the role of female labour in the Muslim economic order.

Many men across the Arab world still feel insulted if one asks them whether their wives work outside the home. In September 1982, as a witness to the census-taking operation in some of the southern and eastern provinces of Morocco, I saw many male heads of households show embarrassment and some shock when questions 18 and 19 of the census questionnaire, concerning women's work outside the home, were asked. 'My wife does not have to work outside; I provide for her. Until my death my wife will not need to work outside.' For these husbands, work by their wives outside the home would represent a disgrace to family honour and would signify their own impotence and failure as males whose duty and identity reside in providing for secluded females.

The effort of the 1982 census planners to assess the state of women's employment was destined to fail for many reasons, chief among them the fact that many Moroccan males perceive a married woman who works outside her home as a potential whore whose husband is an economic failure. The fact that the census data-collection operation typically involved two males – the male head of household (when present) and the census agent, who was likely to be a male primary or secondary school teacher (the census decision-makers did not mobilize women teachers for this task; women are enrolled only as a reserve pool) – made it almost inevitable that the census, in spite of its high cost for both the state and the citizen, would produce an extremely biased image of women's employment needs.

The concept of 'women's work', so banal and overused by development experts at both the national and international levels in our Arab societies, is still a traumatizing idea for many Arab men, particularly those from poorer strata where most women's access to education is hampered, and who view women's work outside the home as an emotional mutilation, a symbolic castration, and whose very sexual identity, their sense of themselves as males, requires that they be the sole economic providers for the family in general and the wife in particular. Women, according to this point of view, cannot have an economic dimension, cannot earn a salary outside the home; that is the privilege and the monopoly of masculinity. These men are not to be condemned for thinking in this way. They are in total harmony with their own frame of reference, the Muslim concept and definitions of masculinity and feminity shaped by *shari'a* laws and values.

This situation raises for social scientists important questions that go far beyond the success or failure of the 1982 Moroccan census – questions about the future of Arab development and economic autonomy.

What are the effects of the integration of the country's economy into the world market and of the introduction of modern technology on the participation of the rural woman in the economy and in other social activities; on her relationship with the community where she lives (in general) and with the family and the husband (in particular); on sex roles, on the sexual division of labour, and, as a result, on the way in which an individual's sex determines the benefits, material (goods or hard cash) and nonmaterial (prestige, respect, etc.), that he or she creates, receives, and/or controls?

This chapter is based largely on the 1981 ILO study mentioned earlier and on a series of interviews conducted between 1977 and 1978 with male executives and personnel staff of factories employing female workers, as well as on my personal observations of the 1982 census data-collection process.[3]

The study tries to assess – beyond the changes in the process of production and the distribution of economic surplus – the nature and scope of the impact of these changes on ideological mechanisms in terms of the redefinition of sex roles.

One of the findings of the ILO research, which examines, among other things, the perception of women's work in peasant families in the rural communities where field work was carried out, is that space is sexually segregated. There is a public and a private space. The public space is male; it is the arena of production, economics, and moneymaking. The private space, on the contrary, is a female space. It is assigned to reproduction and sexuality.

This separation of space into an economic arena (public and male) and a domestic sphere (private and female) also explains one of the findings that the ILO case study brings out – namely, the perception of the woman who works for a wage outside the domestic unit as someone who is taking up unmentionable activities that are seen as prostitution. As she violates the separation of the social fields and transgresses the sexual limits of the division of labour by moving into the economic, public space, she is seen as able to sell only that which she administers as a commodity in the domestic space, in private intimacy – sex.

But, and this is where things start getting complicated, illiterate peasants are not the only ones who confuse women's work outside the home (paid or unpaid, formal or informal) with potential prostitution. Highly trained industrial managers and factory owners as well as technocrats and state planners somehow share this assumption.

Interviews carried out in various textile factories in Rabat and Salé (mostly carpet-weaving units) and sardine-canning units in Assafi between 1978 and 1980 have established that most of the managerial staff, which is exclusively male, expresses at some time or other the idea that 'only loose women go to work outside of their homes.'

As for technocrats and state planners, they seem to have great difficulty in perceiving women's contribution to the national economy. A high percentage of Arab statisticians and economists are conspicuous for a pronounced blindness toward the activity of the female population in the labour force. When one looks at tables listing regions according to the rate of women's activity in the labour force, one is astonished to realize that Arab statisticians perceive and classify the vast majority of Arab women as inactive. In sub-Saharan Africa, the statisticians of the Ivory Coast, Madagascar, Benin, the Central African Republic, Gambia, Liberia, and Mali estimate the rate of activity of women at more than 50 per cent (2 per cent for Algeria, 8 per cent for Morocco, 4 per cent for Tunisia, 3 per cent for Libya, and 5 per cent for Egypt).[4] Could this enormous variation in the reported rate of female participation in the labour force arise because women in North Africa lead a life of leisure and ease? The ILO case study mentioned above proves the contrary. The women peasants never stop saying that their lives are one long chore. Thus, it is only in the Arab statistician's mind that women's inactivity exists.

The planners (whether they are in charge of rural modernization projects, agrarian reform, or creating job opportunities), the statisticians, and the male peasants all share a conviction that is held to some degree by most of the male population, whatever their level of education, income, degree of political maturity, or access to decision-making circles: women are not economic agents; they are domestic agents, and the two identities are mutually exclusive.

The question is, therefore, why do men in modern Arab Muslim societies have great trouble perceiving women's economic dimension? Why is it so difficult for them to *see* women working in extra-familiar space? These questions lead us to a consideration of some of the variables, especially the cultural dimension as manifested in the way Muslim society historically defined sex roles. What was the traditional sexual division of labour in our Arab Muslim societies? Was it different from the present one? If the traditional sexual division of labour is similar to the modern one, how can we explain this absence of change in sex-role perception in an Arab world daily torn by cataclysmic changes in so many other areas?

No one can contest that our Arab society is undergoing rapid and profound transformations (all state planning reflects a wish to be different a few years from now). Some of these changes, such as the digestion of technological know-how and the mastery of its processes, are desired. Other changes, such as runaway Westernization, are opposed and rejected as detrimental to our identity, to our very existence. But our resistance to Westernization does not mean that we stop the process of change. This resistance only intensifies the contradictions and conflicts inherent in change. A Muslim fundamentalist opposes Westernization but daily uses such products of Western civilization as electricity, automative transportation, television, and computers. His resistance therefore only increases the gap between his perception and his behaviour, and thus highlights his inability to control his own life, whence the pertinence of wondering what the clinging to traditional sex roles means in today's dynamic Arab society. How does Islam on the one hand, and history on the other hand, deal with sex-role definitions? Why is the very dynamic Arab world so static when it comes to sex roles?

The ILO study identifies six factors which may have contributed to the lack of recognition of women's economic role. The fact that Arab planners and economists, concerned with optimizing Arab nations' utilization and development of their scarce resources, fail to integrate into their calculations an evaluation of the productive potential of women is attributable at least in part to the following historical influences:

1. The sexual division of labour according to the sacred texts, particularly the Qur'an which regulates daily life.
2. The blossoming of slavery during the Golden Age of the Muslim empire.
3. The climatic conditions of the Mediterranean basin, and particularly its famines and epidemics, which made possible the perpetuation of female slavery until the twentieth century.
4. The aggressive and unregulated introduction of capitalist technology in the colonial period.
5. The petit-bourgeois conceptualization of the woman problem by the Arab nationalist movement both at the end of the nineteenth century and at the beginning of the twentieth.
6. And, finally, the emergence of a petit-bourgeois women's movement after independence and its effects on the perception of women's manual labour in the poorer classes.

This presentation will focus on the first two topics: the sacred text, the Qur'an, and the still powerful image of the *jariya* (female slave during the Muslim Golden Age), considered as overly potent influences on the shaping of sexual identity.

Sex Roles in Medieval Islam

The way in which Islam approached and solved the problem of assigning the place of women is one of the most studied subjects in Muslim society. A superabundance of juridical-religious and pseudo-scientific studies continually reassure the believers about a subject that poses a problem obvious to every person of intelligence: how to reconcile the message of fundamental equality in Muslim doctrine with the specific inequality that is the basis for the relationship of the believer-husband with his believer-wife.

The essential thing to remember for our consideration of the conception of sex roles is that the Qur'an defines these roles very clearly indeed.

The most eloquent formulations are discussed below:

. . . and men are a degree above them [women]. Allah is Mighty, Wise. (Sura II, Verse 228.)[5]

This 'degree above them' has an economic justification; men provide for the needs of women, for women are defined by divine law as not having direct access to material goods. In this sacred division of labour between the sexes, women are defined as incapable of providing for their own needs. This tenet is stated precisely in the following verse:

Men are in charge of women, because Allah hath made the one of them to excel the other, and because they spend of their property [for the support of women]. So good women are the obedient, guarding in secret that which Allah hath guarded. (Sura IV, Verse 34).[6]

This verse is fundamental for the regulation of relations and roles inside the Muslim family; it is at the heart of the majority of the family laws promulgated after the declaration of independence.[7] It is echoed in Article 115 of the Moroccan Family Law promulgated in 1957:

Every human being is responsible for providing for his needs [*nafaqa*] by his own powers except the wife, whose needs will be taken care of by her husband.[8]

Article 118 defines *nafaqa* to mean that which is necessary to satisfy basic vital needs: lodging, food, clothing, and health. It is obvious that Islam clearly defines woman as being above all a sexual agent; she furnishes sexual services and reproduces the human race within the limits of patriarchal legitimacy. The latter imposes on her a chastity which is guaranteed only at the price of a segregation of space that limits the interaction of the wife with any males, except her husband and those who are forbidden to her by the law of incest, and restricts her to a narrow space defined as not economic – domestic space.[9]

The sexual inequality associated with the Qur'an's gender-specific definition of work, which identifies woman as sexual agent and man as provider, is rooted in the memory of the young child, starting with the Qur'anic school, where the child learns writing, language rhythm, and vocabulary through the silken poetry of the sacred book. Every day the Qur'an is read, written, heard, invoked, and practised as law. It is one of the most dynamic forces that has molded the psyche of Muslims of both sexes for more than fourteen centuries.

But the models of hierarchical relationships that the Qur'an imprints in the deepest zones of the Muslim personality would not have retained such influence in the twentieth century had it not been for the expansion of a legendary Muslim empire that allowed sexual inequality to assert itself and to spread through the phenomenon of the *jariya*.

The *Jariya*: History and Legend

Among the best-known books of Muslim literature, and one which (to judge by the number of editions available) is still widely read, is the *Arabian Nights*. Many of the stories in the *Arabian Nights* are situated in Baghdad during the Golden Age of the Muslim empire.[10] There, in the palaces and great houses, powerful men were offered women slaves as today one is offered the loan of a car or any kind of gadget.

> One day Muhammad ibn Sulaiman heard that there was newly arrived in Basrah a fresh batch of young slaves from all countries, so, sitting on his throne among his amirs and the chief nobles of his court, he said to his wazir al-Fadl: 'I wish you to find me a young slave without equal in the whole world. She must have perfect beauty, superior attributes, and an admirably sweet character.'[11]

The wazir went immediately to the slave market, but could find no woman fulfilling the conditions of the king. However, after some days, one of the slave brokers brought news that he had found such a slave as had been requested.

'Bring her quickly to my palace that I may see her,' said the wazir, dismounting from his horse and returning to his apartments. An hour later the broker returned, leading a young girl who was marvellously endowed with swelling breasts, brown lids over night-coloured eyes, smooth full cheeks, a laughing chin just shaded with a dimple, hips in firm curves, a bee's waist, and a heavy swelling croup.[12]

But the potential of Sweet-Friend – for that was her name – did not stop there. Her master, who was selling her, explained to the wazir why he was asking such an exorbitant price for her:

She has had numberless masters; she has learnt the most excellent calligraphy, together with both Arabic and Persian grammar and syntax; she knows the commentaries of the Book, moral law, jurisprudence, philosophy and ethics, geometry, medicine, cadastral survey, and the like; but her chief excellence is in poetry, music of all kinds, singing and dancing.[13]

Instead of turning to the *Arabian Nights*, I could have chosen a Sweet-Friend from one of the authentic history books describing the life of the golden centuries of the Muslim empire, and there are many such books. Passages similar to those cited above can be found, for example, in the twenty volumes of the *Kitab al-Aghani* of Abi al-Faraj al-Asfahani. I purposely chose the *Arabian Nights* because one of the characteristics of the contemporary Muslim psyche is *a confusion between the imaginary and the historical Muslim Golden Age*. And the two coincide perfectly in the key feminine role of the *jariya*, or female pleasure slave.[14] The Muslim believer of the 1980s, overwhelmed by Western technology, is lulled by the thought of this Golden Age when the caliphs of Baghdad ruled the Orient and the Occident and when their power was demonstrated by – among other things – the stream of slaves that flooded the markets of the empire, especially under the Abbasid dynasty:

The *jawari* were very important in the history of Muslim civilization, as important as the male slaves and the 'clients'.[15] The source of the *jawari* were the women and young girls who were captured by the conquerors (Al-Fatihoun calls them 'those who opened the countries to Islam'). They became the property of the conquerors even if they were the daughters of kings. Their conquerors used their labour power and their reproductive capacity, and even sold them. They treated them exactly like objects. As things got better for the Muslims and their property increased, they brought wealth and riches to the treasure-houses of the caliphs and princes, and began to be offered *jawari* as they were offered diamonds and pearls. Whoever wanted to approach a powerful man offered him a *jariya* who excelled in an art which the man particularly appreciated. For example, if he learned that the man loved beauty, he offered him a beautiful slave; if, on the other hand, he discovered that the man who interested him appreciated singing, it was a *jariya* with a melodious voice that he chose. . . .[16]

The author of this passage cites as his references for the section on the *jawari* the great names in the history of that epoch: Ibn Khalikan, al-Asfahani, al-Massoudi, and others.

This period in the history of the Arab Muslim world has played a part – and in our present era of failure and economic dependence still plays a part – in strengthening and maintaining a whole network of models and themes linked to glory, triumph, and economic and political power. The large number of women that one could subjugate, dominate, buy, adorn, be offered, or offer to someone else is one of the symbols that the Muslim Golden Age always associated with success and power. Some centuries later, with the publication of the *Arabian Nights*, this association between success, economic power, and the *jariya* had taken over another terrain besides history to become embedded in the Arab Muslim psyche – and it has taken over the imagination of the fairy-tale world, the dream world.[17]

Moreover, it is the coincidences, the continuities, and the similarities between the sacred models and the historical and imaginary models which are fascinating. For it must not be forgotten that the sacred writings also present an image of women as the source of pleasure through the model of the houri. This model strongly calls to mind the characteristics of the *jariya*. The houri, a female creature in paradise, is supposed to be offered as a reward to believers who have merited access to heaven by their good works on earth. As described in the Qur'an, the houri is beautiful, eternally virgin, and eternally loving:

12. In gardens of delight
15. On gold-embroidered couches,

16. They lie comfortably side by side
17. While young boys made the rounds
18. With bowls and ewers and a cup from a pure spring
19. Wherefrom they get no aching of the head nor any madness,
20. And fruit that they prefer
21. And flesh of fowls that they desire.
22. And [there are] fair ones with wide, lovely eyes,
23. Like unto hidden pearls . . .
35. Lo! We have created them a [new] creation
36. And made them virgins[18],
37. Lovers, friends . . . (Sura XVI.)[19]

This connection between the sacred model of the female (the houri) and the secular models (the historical *jariya* for the Abbasids and the imaginary *jariya* of the *Arabian Nights*) has great importance in sex models and role making in Arab Muslim sexual division of labour. And the two linked models, the sacred and the secular, are associated with success, whether it be success in the beyond or on earth. This pervasive female model is, in my opinion, of utmost importance in explaining, at least partially, the inability of the technocrats, as well as the peasants, to perceive women in any role except a sexual one, or as other than economically subordinate and dependent.

At this point, one must again ask: why is it that in today's dynamic Arab world only medieval models (the Qur'an, the Golden Age legacy of the *jariya* image, etc.) seem to be operational in defining sex roles? Why is it that the eclecticism that reigns in so many spheres of Arab daily life is absent when it comes to the shaping of sexual identity? Why are there not new models competing with the old ones, either imported (e.g., the image of the Western woman working outside of the home) or created by the Arab society itself in its attempt better to control the drastic changes it is undergoing? The fact is that Arab women who were traditionally limited to domestic space have invaded by the millions, especially since World War II, spaces regarded as male: factories, offices, schools, hospitals. Why is it that this incredible change in family structure (the flow of female labour outside of household units) has not been accompanied by a harmonious change in sex role perceptions in our societies? Why is our capacity as Arabs to produce operational models and concepts that better depict our reality, and therefore help us to master it, so inhibited when it comes to relations between the sexes?

To speculate on an answer to this question is to dare to tackle one of the most painful wounds devouring Arab creative energies – our relation to the past, our use of the past, and our consumption of the past. Why do we remain limited to sex-role models that are heavily dependent on our medieval past, instead of creating ones that would help us dynamize our perception of ourselves as sexual beings?

How to deal with the past is one of the questions mobilizing public opinion in the Arab world around the *asala* (authenticity) issue. According to the advocates of *asala*, we, as Arabs, should look to our rich cultural heritage, our centuries-old Muslim tradition, for guidance in shaping our future. The supporters of *asala* drape themselves in a variety of ideological veils; the Muslim fundamentalists, for example, emphasize religious values, while some other believers in *asala* emphasize political ones (often of a xenophobic nature).

My speculative question to the supporters of *asala* is the following: why is it that 'our Arab past', which we are discussing in the 1980s, stops in the ninth century (Christian calendar)? Is not the loss of a single day from a society's awareness of its own history an irredeemable loss? Then why discard from consideration a span of many hundreds of years?

One can speculate, then, that groups claiming that the only 'authentic' cultural heritage comes from the medieval period, are groups which have a vested interest in repudiating all the newer models and cultural frames of reference that appeared in later centuries, and more specifically in recent decades. Laws promulgated in most Arab countries after independence have proclaimed religious law, the *shari'a*, as fixed in the medieval period, to be the guiding light and the source of concepts and principles regulating, in the future, the family and sexual roles and relations. Although many fields of Arab legislation, such as those involving trade and commercial transactions, were liberated from the grip of religious law, family law was one of the few deliberately kept under the medieval sacred text's grip to the exclusion of all other points of view.

The fossilization of the family model and reference basis is a deliberate political choice, one made by a leadership that is threatened in ideological terms by modern models and frames of reference. Models advocating sexual equality would quickly be dismissed as foreign and alien by legislators who use Western-made cars to get to their offices in *shari'a* courts and use all kinds of Western-made technological supplies. It is interesting to note that the Arab leadership's use of the past is selective, and this results in oppressive and anti-egalitarian policies. Much of what was gained in the Arab world's struggle for liberation has been carefully buried and rejected as heretical. In particular, the traditional model of the division of labour has been retained because of the benefits it offers to whomever buys female labour on the national labour market or sells it on the international labour market. Not acknowledging that women's work outside the home is a legitimate right enables whoever uses female labour to pay a lower price for it, so that female labour is the cheapest and most easily exploitable form of labour in our countries. Ideological choices are never accidental. Whence comes the need to investigate who profits in Arab economies from supposedly 'modern' economic and statistical tools so efficient in masking woman's work and its monetary value and so similar in this respect to medieval perceptions of woman's role and place in society.

Notes

1.   Fatima Mernissi, *Développement capitaliste et perceptions des femmes dans la société arabo-musulmane: une illustration des paysannes du Gharb Maroc.* The study was prepared for the Tripartite Seminar of the International Labour Office for Africa on 'The Place of Women in Rural Development' held in Dakar. Senegal, June 15-19, 1981. This study has been translated into English by *Feminist Issues,* a journal published in Berkeley, CA, in their Fall 1982 issue and Spring 1983 issue.

For a clarification of the concept of women's work see Fadela Bennis, 'La prise en compte du travail domestique par la théorie économique', in 'Approches du travail féminin', Mémoire de D.E.S. en sciences économiques. (Rabat: Faculté de Droit, Juillet 1983.)

2.   See F. Mernissi, 'The Regulation of Female Sexuality in the Muslim Social Order', in *Beyond the Veil* (Cambridge, MA: Schenkman Publishing Co., 1975).

3.   The results of the 1977-78 study on crafts are still unpublished and are available in the Rabat Faculty of Letters. Fifty students, with Mohammed Guessous and myself as supervisors, covered most of the crafts within the Rabat-Salé area – both modern factories and domestic units. Both workers, mostly females, and manager, mostly males, were interviewed. The data are in Arabic.

As for the 1982 census, I covered 4,000 kilometres in rural Morocco with another sociologist, Malika Belghiti, as a team hired by the Ministry of Planning to observe household heads' reaction to the census questionnaire. The field report where the sexual dynamics emerged as one of the obstacles hampering the scientific process could be obtained from the Secretariat of the Moroccan Ministry of Planning. The title is 'Evaluation critique du Questionnaire du Recensement Général de la population et de l'habitat, 1982'.

4.   'Les Femmes dans la société', *Peuples* 7, No. 4 (1980).

5.   *The Glorious Koran,* a bilingual edition with English translation, Introduction and Notes by Marmaduke Pickthall. (Albany, NY: State University of New York Press, 1976), pp. 44-45.

6.   *The Glorious Koran,* p. 104.

7.   Since the end of the 19th century, much of the reasoning of conservative Arab political circles has been based on this verse. It must be added that, within these circles, the Qur'an is implicitly considered a book that only the believer of the male sex can read and interpret. From this it follows logically that a female citizen of a Muslim society does not have the right to interpret the Qur'an; if she does, it is blasphemy. Nowadays, according to prevailing conservative authorities, women are to be excluded from knowledge of science – an exclusively male privilege; they are relegated to the position of sex object and considered to lack

reason. The conservatives consider the *umma* (the Muslim community) to be an entity consisting exclusively of responsible members of the male sex, because only they are endowed with reason. Thus the notion that a woman could claim the right, as a citizen of the *umma*, to interpret the Qur'an, which governs her life, throws into question the whole comfortable universe that the conservatives have constructed. The future of the *umma* depends on what choices are made concerning this right to the interpretation of the great problem that agitates the Arab world – the problem of democracy. The question is thus one of a very simple application or rejection of the principle of democracy – namely, do all the members of the *umma*, whatever their sex, have the right to interpret the Qur'an, or do only men have that right? The right to interpret reality is precisely the right that women claim. Like the Qur'an, economic and statistical knowledge today is used by a predominantly male technocracy to interpret the reality of all people – including that of women.

8.   *Dhahir*, No. 1-57-343, published in *Bulletin official*, No. 2354, December 6, 1957.

9.   It must be recalled that sexual inequality as a foundation of monotheistic religion is scarcely peculiar to Islam. Islam shares this characteristic with the two great religions (from which it issued and which it claims as source and reference – Judaism and Christianity. In these two latter religions the degradation of women is much more virulent, at the level of principle, than it is in Islam. This aspect of Judeo-Christianity has been considered in great detail, especially by feminist studies. The female figure of the Virgin Mary is a mutilated woman who reproduces without the sexual act. In order to give birth while remaining a virgin, a woman, in Mary's circumstances, must undergo transformations in the Christian psyche which are just as mutilating as the spatial immobilization in the Muslim universe. Arguments intended to prove that Christianity, or Judaism, treats women better than Islam scarcely interest me as a woman. These are debates which interest men and reflect their concerns. A consensus seems to have emerged from feminist studies around the world in the last decade that monotheistic religions based on the inferior position of women constitute one of the mainstays of their degradation. See, for example, papers presented at 12-18 June 1983 conference organized by Harvard Center for the Study of World Religions on 'Women, Religion and Social Change'.

10.   The Abbasid dynasty replaced the Umayyad dynasty around the middle of the 8th century. It transferred the capital of the Muslim empire from Damascus to Baghdad, which became the capital in 763 A.D.

11.   *The Book of the Thousand and One Nights*, rendered into English from the literal and complete French translation of Dr. J. C. Mardrus by Powys Mathers (London: George Routledge & Sons, 1947), Vol. 1, p. 370. (Although the title of this edition is a literal translation of the Arabic title, this work is commonly referred to in English as the *Arabian Nights*.)

12.   Ibid., 1:371.

13.   Ibid., 1:373.

14.   The usage of the word *jariya* varied in different epochs and different regions. This variation is not really relevant here because, in the centuries of Muslim expansion and cultural flowering, the word was synonymous with *slave of the female sex*. The plural of *jariya* is *jawari*.

15.   The clients (*al-mawali*) were linked to powerful men by a system of

patronage, of clientage, which gave them a special status, distinct from the status of a slave.

16.   Jurji Zaydan, *Tarikh al-tamaddun al-Islam*) [The History of Islamic Civilization], Vol. 5, p. 35 (n.pub.). The translation from Arabic to English is that of the author.

17.   The *Arabian Nights* is a work of very mysterious origin. The author, or more probably authors, is unknown. It is a veritable mosaic with the style and power of a popular creation, the distillation of a whole culture, a whole civilization. The work existed only in manuscript form up until the nineteenth century. A first printed edition appeared in Calcutta in 1814-18. The Cairo edition of Bulaq did not appear until 1835.

18.   'Them' here refers to the believers who have gained access to Paradise.

19.   *The Glorious Koran*, pp. 713-14.

CHAPTER VIII

The *Jariya* and the Caliph[1]
Thoughts on the Place of Women in
Muslim Political Memory

We are living through a transitional period in our civilization in which Islam and its tradition are appealed to as a philosophical justification for inequality, including sexual inequality. Every text which asserts sexual equality without ambiguity, as does the Universal Declaration of Human Rights, is said to be a violation of the Muslim heritage, both in the spirit and the letter. The legitimacy of democracy as the basis of legislation and as the fundamental value of the modern Muslim state is thus currently contested in the name of an allegedly sexist Muslim memory. Democracy based on the Universal Declaration of Human Rights, which many Muslim countries have signed as a basic text, does not, by definition, brook any exception to the principle of the equality of citizens. Now, it is claimed that the place of woman in the Muslim tradition is either non-existent or subaltern. Modern Muslim men are thus faced with a momentous choice. They must either betray their ancestors by asserting the equality of the sexes or betray 150 million Muslim women by depriving them of their effective rights. Is there another, third way which would permit of a reconciliation between the past and modernity?

Pertinence of the Problematic and
Definition of Concepts

What is the modern Muslim male's responsibility to his past and his 'political memory'?

If Muslim man has inherited a memory in which inequality has governed human relations, is he still the prisoner of that memory in 1989? To reply to that question is in itself to choose one's future and, particularly, the place one wishes to occupy among the nations. Given the incredible advance of democracy both in Eastern Europe and that also marked the year 1989 with the Chinese people, the largest in the world, taking to the streets to campaign on its behalf, the path towards equality seems to be the one the comity of nations has chosen. Is the Arab male going to set himself apart by posing as the defender of inequality? That choice is always open to him. But he who, not so long ago, was in the forefront of the world's peoples, will be condemned to be the standard-bearer of all that is archaic and outdated if he does so. The situation today is not unlike the early years of this century. The great nations had already abolished slavery, but the Muslim leaders did so only under compulsion from their colonial rulers. Might it be said that 'Muslim political memory' is one in which time is arbitrarily arrested at what is known as the 'Golden Age', the age of the Abbasids and of slavery? Do those who speak in the name of Islam call only on a selectively limited version of the tradition? Why should that tradition not take in the most recent human advances made in the nineteenth and twentieth centuries?

Does the Muslim memory, which currently refuses to grant women the full range of their rights as citizens, reject the abolition of slavery as part of its heritage for the mere reason that it was imposed by France and Britain, the then colonial powers? In the struggle for rights and equality for all, which is the defining feature of the modern history of the last three centuries, Muslims have scarcely played a pioneering role. They have, rather, been people frightened by progress and wedded to outmoded ways. In spite of Islam's declared opposition to slavery, Muslim leaders have refused to outlaw it within their territories, when the – supposedly inhuman – Christian nations condemned it. Though France abolished slavery in all its overseas territories by a decree of the Second Republic on 27 April 1848, it was not abolished in Tunisia until May 1890 and in Egypt in 1898. In Morocco, we had to wait until 1922 to see it abolished, when it was in fact done so only by a circular of the French colonial administration. In 1951, Yemen and Saudi Arabia were still refusing to respond to United Nations questionnaires on the state of slavery within their borders, which they regarded as an unwarranted interference in their internal affairs.[2] Forty years later, in the 1990s, those who speak in the name of Islam talk in the same terms where women are concerned. There is good reason, then, for us to look closely at this memory they call upon to legitimize inequality.

Problematic

What is the 'normal' place the tradition reserves for women in the 'political memory'?

The triumph of Mrs Benazir Bhutto in the 1988 elections and her appointment as Prime Minister of Pakistan gave the advocates of the exclusion of women from politics a chance to cry blasphemy and degeneracy. We may cite the Islamic Democratic Alliance (IDA) and its leader Mr Nawaz Sharif, and Mr Khan Junejo, a member of the Muslim League (ML) and a former minister of Zia al-Haq as examples. In an effort to prevent the appointment of Mrs Bhutto, they argued that a woman cannot accede to the office of head of state in a Muslim nation.

Muslim memory is a vast accumulation of fifteen centuries of diverse cultural experiences, of struggles between rulers and the ruled, of popular campaigning movements variously held in check, and more or less despotic responses to those movements. To take Muslim history as a reference is, therefore, necessarily to select, prioritize and choose from among the fund of images, models, clichés and schemas swept along in the history of a great people, no single precise vision of which has to be accepted. Every generation draws from that fund what it needs to manufacture its 'cultural identity' according to the pressing problems facing it. 'Islamic memory' is, therefore, the product of a choice like any other. And the proof of this is that this memory varies from one social class to another. The official Islam of the ulemas of the cities differs from the Islam of the peasants, who come in their thousands to Shaikh al-Kamel at Meknès. The 'Muslim memory' varies so much between classes that the popular Islam of sects and trances is rejected and condemned as heretical by the Islam of the middle classes and the town-dwellers. Since memory is a choice, why choose a memory in which women have no right to equality? Who are these Muslims discomfited by equality? To answer that question, a countrywide sociological investigation should be carried out on a representative sample of the population. And this would be very easy, since such a study would not have to involve more than a thousand people.

While we wait for our politicians to take up this question to the extent of deciding to devote research funding to it, we can always investigate 'written memory'. This is a less burdensome task, but just as pertinent. What is the natural 'role' of women registered in the memory of our ancestors? One reading of classical Arab history, which is by definition aristocratic since only the palaces had their historians and were the centre of that history, is that the 'natural' place of a woman is that of a *jariya*, a slave whose essential function is to obey.

Before presenting the results of this research, some conceptual definitions and methodological clarifications are called for. First of all, what is 'political memory'? How can it be extracted from fifteen centuries of an Islam which includes within it several different cultures? And what memory are we going to take as constitutive of Muslim identity – that of the leaders of the Empire or of those contesting that leadership? The memory of the poor or the memory of the rich? Of men or women? Of Arabs or Berbers, Kurds, Zanj (Sudanese blacks) etc.

'Muslim Political Memory': A chronicle of the life of the Caliph

This chapter draws on the writings of classical historians like Ibn Sa'ad, Tabari, Mas'udi, Ibn al-Athir, etc., who are all men, describing events from the point of view of order and those whose duty it is to uphold it. The concept of *tarikh* (chronicled history) is a reductive one: only chronicles of the lives of rulers and their entourages have come down to us. The books of *tarikh* which are, nonetheless, constitutive of the tradition, and the authors of which (such as those quoted above) are recognized as having written 'classics' – as dependable sources and proper references – are the product of a highly political choice, referring, as they do, to the social or economic life of the people (*nass*) and of the nation (*umma*) only as a marginal and secondary matter.[3] Only the caliphs, princes, sultans and their courts (particularly the vizirs) are actors in this *tarikh*. In the eleven volumes of the *Tarikh al-umam wa al-muluk* of Tabari or the *Muruj al-dhahab* of Mas'udi [translated into French as *Les Prairies d'Or*], the history of Muslim society is reduced to a chronicle of political events in the narrow sense of the term: which caliph replaced which, who conquered what territory, the appointment of governors, the raising of taxes and, lastly, the names of the leaders of rebellions, the *zindigs* (heretics), who led the protest movements, and their elimination. Those movements were often religious in character, as was the case with the Shi'a, the Kharijites etc. We might say that one of the tasks incumbent on modern intellectuals is to write the as yet hidden side of our history, that side in which the actors are the common people, craftsmen and women, tradesmen and women who produced the wealth of the Empire. Since that has not yet been done, it is this *tarikh*, this truncated history we shall keep to here as our 'Muslim Political Memory'. But even this *tarikh*, stunted as it is by the absence of the people, treats the subject of women differently in different periods. Yet only the Abbasid era is accorded priority. Our reading, then, will limit itself to the first centuries of Islam and will privilege this Abbasid era (750–945) which is still powerfully evocative. We do this to bring out one of the paradoxes of Muslim memory, namely the pre-eminence of women on the political stage in the first decades and the decline of their position under the Umayyads and the Abbasids. We must distinguish between three periods.

The first of these, the epic years of Islam, is the age of the Prophet and the orthodox caliphs in which women became pre-eminent on the political stage as disciples of the Prophet. This period begins with the first year of the *hijra* (622 AD) and ends with Mu'awiya I's seizure of power in year 41 of the *hijra* (661).

The second period, some generations later, after the death of the disciples, is one in which the women of the Arab aristocracy were to take centre stage in the caliph's entourage. They were to figure prominently in the historical record as wives and mothers of caliphs and princes. This period coincides with the first Umayyads and the consolidation of the Empire.

The third period ushers in the triumph of the *jawari* with the Abbasids. These female slaves, reduced by their very status to the role of courtesans, will be the only women allowed to stand out in the caliph's entourage.

Already, then, as we shall see, the Muslim who wishes to condemn women to marginality chooses his historical period well. It is not the period of the Prophet he chooses, but that of Abbasid despotism!

Triumph of women as disciples during the epic years of Islam: partners in the political game

The important place accorded to women throughout the first decades of Islam is shown in the history books. The stars of the piece, so to speak, are the Prophet's wives and the female disciples who occupied the place of honour. The historians describe the Prophet's entourage, his wives such as Khadija, A'isha, Umm Salma, Zaynab Bint Jahsh, or his disciples, many of whom belong to the Quraysh nobles. They depict a political scene in which the women are independent and make demands.

The Prophet is described listening to women and attentive to their complaints. Two examples are quite revealing in this regard. The first of these is the case of Umm Salma, who questioned the Prophet as to the meaning of the revealed word: 'How is it,' she asks the Prophet one day, 'that you men should be mentioned in the Qur'an while we are ignored?'[4] Her question is heard and a reply given, with reference to the famous verse 25 of Sura 48 (The Victory) which acknowledges women's status as implied equal partners with men in the process of revelation ('believers, both men and women'). The Qur'an is addressed to all and women are, therefore, responsible, like men, for the triumph of Islam on earth and for their acts before God in the hereafter. According to this verse, women, Tabari tells us, have a right to pardon for their sins and a right to Paradise.[5] The example of Khawlah Bint Ta'laba is also symbolic in some measure of the pre-eminence of women on the political stage – in particular in the dialogue between the divine and the community. Speaking through his Prophet, Allah replies to a woman who is upset by the behaviour of her husband, and the female disciple becomes the object of the verse: 'God hath heard the words of her who pleaded with thee against her husband, and made her plaint to God.' ('*Qad sami'a Allahu qawla al-lati tujadulika fi zawjiha wa tashtaki ila Allah*'). Overwhelmed by her marital problems, Khawlah had gone to see the Prophet to put her case to him. He advised her to await the revelation which would indicate the course to follow.[6] These two examples are sufficient to give an idea of the presence of women in the arena of politics and the nature of their relationship with political power. The women ask questions as persons concerned in the political game, i.e. in the management of relations between believers, and between these latter and the sources of authority – in this case, divine authority. And the divine one, as the supreme authority, responds to their questioning. Paradoxically, this marvellous moment in our history, when God and the Prophet lend an ear to the weak, and to women among them, is hardly evoked at all today as constitutive of 'our' memory.

Under the Prophet and the first four orthodox caliphs (from year 11 to year 40 of the *hijra*), primacy in the chronicles of the historians reverted to the Mothers of the Believers, a title granted to the wives of the Prophet (*ummahat al-muminin*), and to the disciples (*as-sahabiya*). History accords them enormous importance. This can be seen in the biographies of the disciples such as the *Tabaqat* of Ibn Sa'd, *Usd al-ghaba* of Ibn al-Athir or Ibn Hajar's *al-Isaba* . Each of these writers devoted a volume to the women.[7] The same is true of works devoted specifically to religious history. In the thirty volumes of the *Tafsir* of al-Tabari, a commentary on the Qur'an setting each verse in context and a magisterial portrayal of the historical conditions of the revelation and the actors involved in each of the conflicts which arose, women seem actively involved and are depicted as performing responsibly and as being given full responsibility. They play a considerable part in the various conflicts and are far from passive and obedient. They argue as disciples of the Prophet and call others to account.[8] And the strongest proof that Allah and his Prophet inaugurated Islam as a great paean to equality in the 7th century is that, at that point, women had access to the highest status, the status of disciples (*sahabiyat*). A few decades later, with the accession to power, after the orthodox caliphs, of the Umayyads, the women of the Arab aristocracy were to take over. As independent, demanding and proud as their predecessors, they would consolidate their own rights – especially the right not to wear the veil – and to contest their husbands' rights to polygamy.

Rejection of polygamy and the veil under the first Umayyads

Unlike the later Umayyads and the Abbasids, who were to prefer *jawari*, slaves, as their wives and the mothers of their children, the first Umayyads kept up the Arab tradition of marriage between aristocrats. The measure of a woman's nobility was her pride and her capacity to defy men in a position of authority. Women's protests were focused on two institutions which they rejected: the veil and polygamy.

The most representative leading figures of this movement were the two great ladies of the Arab nobility, women of rare beauty who are mentioned without fail in all the chronicles: Sakina Bint al-Hussein and Ai'sha Bint Talha. Sakina Bint al-Hussein, the granddaughter of the Prophet,[9] had won fame by forcing monogamy upon her third husband, the grandson of the Caliph 'Uthman Ibn 'Affar. She even forbade him to approach another woman, including his own *jawari*, and did not allow him to go against the least of her desires.[10] She divorced him amid great scandal when she caught him red-handed with none other than one of his 'legitimate' *jawari*, owned in accordance with the prescribed rules. The historical documents all stress the fact that Sakina was *barzaa*, i.e. unveiled. She was present at the death of her father at Karbala, and used to attend the mosque escorted by his *jariya* and harangue the Imam if he dared to attack 'Ali in his preaching.

The other great celebrity of the time was Ai'sha Bint Talha, a contemporary of Sakina's and, like her, an aristocrat, the niece of Ai'sha Bint Abi Bakr, the wife of the Prophet.[11] She too refused to wear the veil. She explained that if God had created her so beautiful, He had not done so for her to be hidden from sight.[12]

With the last Umayyads,[13] the influence of the *jariya* began to show in the political chronicles and it became clearly marked under the Abbasids. As the classical historians, Tabari, Mas'udi or Ibn al-Athir employ chronological order, first the retinues of female disciples (including the wives of the Prophet), then the aristocratic Arab women gradually leave the political stage. In the second century of the *hijra*, the women of the aristocracy disappear from the lives of the caliphs and from the historical chronicles.

Five or six generations later, they are being replaced by interminable processions of *jawari*. The best known of these were Ghadir, the *jariya* of the Caliph al-Hadi; 'Arib, the *jariya* of the Caliph al-Ma'mun; Farida ('the Great'), *jariya* of Harun al-Rashid; Fadl and Mahbouba, *jawari* of al-Mutawakkil who had a whole collection of them.[14] These women were talented, possessing musical and poetic gifts and beauty, but what they did not have was the capacity to assert themselves in any other way than as courtesans. Their status as slaves kept them in a precarious position. Their status as favourites, which was by definition ephemeral, made it impossible for them to make any demands. Their privileges were also unstable. They had to build a life upon seduction, cunning and diplomacy. They acquitted themselves with great brio in their roles as subordinates, making submission to the caliph's whim their very *raison d'être*. And so they handed down to us an image, which we know today in the *Thousand and One Nights*, in which love, seduction and enslavement are forever linked in our imaginations. From this point on, on the political stage, women were no longer anything but courtesans.

The triumph of the Jariya under the Abbasids

It is always instructive to seek out the linguistic roots of words. What is a *jariya*? According to the *Lisan al-'Arab* dictionary, it is something in movement, something which moves. It is, at one and the same time, the wind, the star and the ship. But it is also the emissary (*rasul*) and the servant (*khadim*).[15] Another synonym of *jariya* is *qina*, which al-Jahiz employs as the title for his extraordinary *Risala fi al-kayan* (essay on slave women), in which he attempts to understand the fascination they exerted on men.[16] *Qina* is synonymous with *jariya* and the two words are, moreover, used interchangeably. In *qina*, the notion of slavery is present. Ibn Manzur, the author of the dictionary, tells us that the *qina* is a slave, whether she is a singer or not. He adds, 'If the name *qina* is given to a *jariya* who knows the art of singing, this is precisely because that art is practised only by slaves, and not at all by free women'.

How does one become a *jariya* or a *qina*? How does one become a slave? One is a slave when one has been bought in a market. The most commonly used means for obtaining slaves was *sabya*, the capturing of the women and children of the enemy in the act of war. The prisoners of war of the vanquished enemy (*asra*) became slaves. Ibn Manzur puts matters simply: '*al-saby* is to reduce people to slavery'. A *sabya* woman is a captured woman. She is part of the spoils of war.

With the expansion of the Empire under the Umayyads, and particularly under the Abbasids, military conquests brought *jawari* from all conquered lands on to the markets of Damascus and Baghdad. There were Africans, Asians and Europeans among them. The only women to elude the Muslim Empire were American Indians.

However, and this is the detail which interests us here, the arrival of *jawari* in enormous numbers changed the ways of the court. Whereas the first caliphs were proud of their wives, who came, like them, from aristocratic stock, soon the opposite was true and the princes were under the spell of the *jawari*. 'There was no caliph and no figure possessing similar power or means who did not have by him a slavegirl to drive away flies and fan him, whilst another served him, and all this before the public'.[17] Yet, they were not content to use these girls merely for their labour and for entertainment, but raised them to the ranks of wives and mothers.

Though a caliph born of an aristocratic mother was something rare at the beginning of the Umayyad dynasty, the opposite was soon to be the case. However, Ibn Hazm sums up the later situation thus: 'Among the Abbasids, only three caliphs were sons of a *hurra* (free woman) and among the Umayyads of Andalusia not a single son of a free woman ever succeeded in becoming caliph.'[18] The majority of caliphs had slave mothers of foreign extraction – Berbers, Turks, Romans, Kurds etc.

The place of the *jariya* on the caliphal scene was such that soon a new literary genre appeared, devoted to the description of the *jawari*, examples of which are the works of Abu al-Faraj al-Isbahani and al-Suyuti.[19]

What was the mystery behind the fascination of caliphs and men of power for the *jawari*? Historians, thinkers, philosophers and other writers have attempted to understand their incredible success. From al-Jahiz to Ahmad Amin, the author of *Duha al-Islam*, many reasons for this have been suggested. Some say that the *jawari* were more experienced sexually since they learned the arts of love from several different partners. Others put their success down to the attraction of exoticism: the *jawari* brought with them their foreign culture and new models of refinement. The Indian, Persian, Roman and Ethiopian women dazzled the Arab caliphs with music, singing, caresses, perfumes, tales of distant lands and so many things previously unknown to them.[20] Al-Jahiz explains that, with the *jariya*, the master could have sexual relations and then sell her on if she did not please him. With the free woman, we are told, he was trapped. But this is a bogus argument in a society where the caliph and any good believer had the right to repudiate his wife, whether or not she was an aristocrat, by thrice pronouncing the phrase '*anti talik*' (you are repudiated). The obvious reason for the *jariya*'s success, which none of the authors I have mentioned lights upon, is easily explained: with her, the man was by definition superior. She was merely his slave.

The sexual experience of the *jawari* and their musical talents were, assuredly, important factors. But we know from the historical documents that Sakina Bint al-Hussein and A'isha Bint Talha were peerless lovers with their husbands.[21] Their cries of pleasure are done full justice by the historians, who were fascinated by these women in whom the four inseparable criteria for seductiveness were united: pride in being an Arab, physical beauty, and, most importantly, quick-wittedness and the inclination to *nushuz* – the capacity to challenge the husband's authority and rebel against it. The more powerful the husbands, the less they could cope with the challenge of these indomitable women. According to the historical sources, Sakina had five or six husbands.

Ahmad Amin has claimed that foreign women were more beautiful than the Arabs. It is odd to see such an expert, whose purpose is not the mere chronicling of events but analysis, forgetting that beauty is ideologically determined. In Morocco in 1960, a good-looking man was said to be as 'handsome as a sherif'. At the end of the eighties, we say: 'He is as handsome as an American'. The adverts for Coca-Cola depicting blond athletes romping about in the sea and Friday night films have certainly played a considerable part in this. It is not by chance that in the adverts on Moroccan TV ordinary women appear in adverts for Butagaz and pressure cookers, but are never seen in banks and computer showrooms. Moroccan banks have allowed themselves to be convinced that the right way to sell themselves is through the cosmopolitan poses and languid gazes of the Casablancan bourgeoisie. Nothing is more political than taste and seduction. Nothing is less natural than the kind of man a woman finds attractive and vice versa. I often ask my Indian, Japanese or French friends when they are visiting Morocco to point out in cafés or on the beach those Moroccans they find handsome, judging by their own canons of beauty. The men and women they identify as attractive are never those a Moroccan would have chosen. The success of the *jariya* cannot, therefore, be explained by the aesthetic criteria of the period.

What were the reasons for this sudden turnabout? Three generations after the Prophet, ideal beauty was an Arabic, aristocratic beauty. Four generations later, the Arab caliphs who dominated the world no longer saw themselves reflected in their compatriots. They sought beauty elsewhere, among slave-women. Seduction is a very complex business, but we know from the study of the more recent history of Morocco that there is an intimate connection between what is regarded as beautiful and the prevailing political relations of force. It is no accident that the members of the early Moroccan nationalist élite, who studied in France in the 1940s and were to be found in the key posts in the government and civil service after Independence, were under the spell of French women. Many of the ministers of that period had French wives. The case of Morocco on the eve of Independence is an interesting one, since the infatuation for foreign women among the élite did not last long. From the 1970s onwards, the technocrats of the Moroccan state fell under the spell of the beautiful women of Tangiers, Tetuan and, most especially, Casablanca. The men in power found Moroccan nationals attractive – well-qualified, ambitious women sitting astride two cultures and juggling two languages: French and Arabic. The technocrats and businessmen of the eighties, and nineties are part of a new generation of bourgeoisie very different from the old nationalist élite and much less in thrall to France.

None of those opposed to the election of Benazir Bhutto in Pakistan recalled the political power exercised by women in the early days of Islam. Why did the *jawari* have so much success in the days of the caliphs and why does that success continue today? Why are we still being called on to play the role of *jariya*? Why does no good Muslim wish to liberate us by looking back to the Prophet's splendid days at Medina, when women took part, as disciples, in the building of an initially egalitarian Islam?

The cult of courtesans in 'political memory' reflects our nostalgia for absolutism
Being myself a woman of Fez and owing much to the very pragmatic traditions of that city, I believe we have to take another look at the key factor in the *jariya* success story. The caliphs preferred the *jawari* because they obeyed more readily than a *hurra* (free woman). Obeying was the *jariya*'s function. That was what she was bought for. And those who argue, in the name of the Muslim tradition, that our role in the political arena is to obey, not to lead, draw for this on a very precise period in Muslim history, the Golden Age, the age of absolutism which began with Mu'awiyah. We know that Mu'awiyah seized power by violence and, against the will of the Prophet, made the transmission of that power dynastic. The infatuation with the *jariya* was in fact a manifestation of the despotic nature of power. A simple anecdote, related by al-Jahiz, well illustrates this: 'When a young slave was brought to Mu'awiyah, he stripped her of her clothing before his friends, laid his riding crop across her lap (*yad'u al-qadip 'ala rakabiha* – *qadip* is also a vulgar form for penis) and, if he found the flesh firm, announced that this was "solid stuff". Then, addressing Sa'sa'a bnou Suhan, he added that he should "take her for one of his sons, as it was not lawful for Yazid (his own son) to have her after what he had done".'[22]

However, if Mu'awiyah prepared the ground for one of the most despotic concentrations of power in universal history, the man who perfected the system, to the point where his name alone is still powerfully evocative, was Harun al-Rashid. And once again, his relationship with one of his favourites, Zaat al-Khaal, is revealing of the symbolism of the *jariya*. The confusion of love and whim here, of submission with favours and access to wealth, is clear for all to see.

Zaat al-Khaal, literally the woman with the beauty spot, was very beautiful and talented. She was the *jariya* of the famed Ibrahim al-Mawsili, the greatest artist of his day. He taught her the art of song and composed poems in which he lauded her charms. She became famous, sufficiently so indeed for Harun al-Rashid to wish to possess her. He bought her from Ibrahim. On one evening of very great intimacy, at the height of his passion, Harun al-Rashid, seized by a pang of jealousy over Zaat al-Khaal's past, questioned her. He demanded the truth on a question which was tormenting him: had she had relations with her teacher and former master, Ibrahim al-Mawsili? The *jariya* thought for an hour then, in a noble gesture in which love of truth won out over fear of punishment, she gave her reply: 'Yes, once only,' she replied to Harun al-Rashid, who took it very badly. And yet Ibrahim had been within his rights since the *jariya* belonged to him.

Harun al-Rashid, beside himself with jealousy, rejected Zaat al-Khal. To punish her, he offered her to his slave, Hamawiya. One day, however, he again felt a desire to see her once more. He told Hamawiya he was longing to hear Zaat al-Khal sing. 'We shall come to you tomorrow, Sire,' the slave replied. In order to do justice to the situation, Hamawiya rushed to the jeweller and hired from him the precious stones and pearls which Zaat al-Khaal had been accustomed to wear when she was at the palace.

When Harun al-Rashid saw her, he was once again captivated by her beauty, but also immediately jealous of a slave capable of adorning his *jariya* with such finery. Forgetting the beauty, Harun al-Rashid enquired after the origin of the jewels: 'How can you give such jewels?' he asked Hamawiya. 'How can you bestow such gifts when I haven't yet appointed you governor?' Terror-stricken, Hamawiya confessed that they were merely loaned to him. Al-Rashid, reassured as to the honesty of his slave and, more importantly, as to his poverty, which was the mark of his inferior status, summoned the jeweller, bought the jewels for Zaat al-Khaal and promised to grant her, there and then, any wish she might express. And what did she ask? That he appoint Hamawiya governor of Persia and give him the taxes of that country for seven years. Al-Rashid kept his promise.[23]

The story of Zaat al-Khaal tells us as much about the political nature of Harun al-Rashid's power as it does about Zaat al-Khaal. She employed her powers of seduction to obtain a political favour. Her request that her protector be granted the governorship of Persia, one of the most important nations of the Empire, evidently does not violate the system but respects its rules. In playing the role of courtesan, the *jariya* symbolizes and reflects the key value of the whole edifice – caprice. In acceding to her request, Harun al-Rashid reveals the principles by which his empire was governed.

Conclusion:
What is to be Done with an Anti-democratic 'Political Memory'?

We might say that those who contest women's entitlement to their political rights in the name of Muslim memory have selected from that memory the period of absolutism's heyday, as embodied in and symbolized by the figure of the *jariya*.

Those women were kept submissive. Courtesans like Zaat al-Khaal did not disturb the political arena in the least. Indeed, they fitted into it perfectly, knowing the rule and following it to the letter. And the rule was: anything can be obtained by begging it as a favour. But no demands must ever be made. Caprice rules the universe. Silence, on the one hand, and manipulation, on the other, are the only possible forms of political participation.

Every claiming of Islam as a tradition is a political act. Every 'tradition' is a political construct, a sophisticated editing of 'memory' which reinforces the speaker's interests. Muslim men who wish to live democratically would have no difficulty in unearthing from the past Muslim women who were partners in the game of politics, such as the Prophet's wives and disciples. Whilst those whom the advent of egalitarian participation discomfits could always point to the example of the courtesans in the rulers' palaces.

It is crucial for any great civilization like Islam, which has been in decline for centuries and today wishes to take its place once again within the comity of nations, analytically to examine and decipher its memory in order to be able to transcend it and use it as a force that carries it forward. And Islam, as a vast and wide-ranging civilization, enables us to choose from within it to be as democratic as the Prophet was. A past is always interesting insofar as it allows us to develop a different present. The creativity which characterizes the writings on the first decades of Islam, the years of the Prophet and his disciples, derives precisely from the fact that the Islam of that period was that of the deprived and the persecuted – the Islam of those rejected by aristocratic, slave-owning Mecca. The Islam of Medina was a moment in which hierarchies and fortunes were destabilized. In their demands, their pride and their concern with the politics of community affairs, the female disciples embodied hope for the emergence of a more egalitarian world. And wherever we see an egalitarian world in gestation, women are always the first who are working to bring it about.

Notes

1.   This chapter was inspired by the study of the historical texts for the book *The Forgotten Queens of Islam* (Cambridge: Polity Press, 1993), first published in French by Albin Michel in Paris and Éditions le Fennec in Casablanca in Spring 1990. Its central theme is women and political power.

2.   See the entry *"abd"* by R. Brunschvig in *Encyclopaedia of Islam*, Vol. I (Leiden/London, 1960), pp. 36-7.

3.   Al-Mas'udi, *Muruj al-dhahab* (4 volumes), (Beirut: Dar al-Ma'rifa, 1983) (French translation, *Les Prairies d'Or* by A. C. Barbier de Meynard and A. J.-B. Pavet de Courteille, Société Asiatique, Paris, 1971) – the author died in A.H. 356 (10th century); al-Tabari, Abu Jafar Muhammad Ibn Jarir, *Tarikh al-umam wa al-muluk* (13 volumes). (Beirut: Dar al-Fikr, 1979) – the author died in A.H. 310 (10th century AD); Ibn al-Athir, *al-Kamil fi al-tarikh* (9 volumes) (Beirut: Dar al-Mashriq, n.d.) – the author died in the year 630 of the *hijra* (13th century).

4.   Tabari, *Tafsir, jami 'al-bayan 'an ta' wil ayi al-qur'an* (Beirut: Dar al-Fikr, 1984 edition), Vol. XXII, p. 10; subsequently referred to as *Tafsir*.

5.   *Tafsir*, Vol. XXII, p. 9.

6.   For a brief and concise reference, see *'Umar Kahhala, A'lam al-nisa' fi 'almay al-'Arabi wa al-Islami* (Famous women in the Muslim and Arab worlds) (Damascus: Mu'assasat al-risala, 1982), p. 382; author's introduction dated 1959. Kahwlah is also referred to in Ibn Sa'ad's *Tabaqat* and in the biographies of disciples such as Ibn Hajar's *Al-Isaba* and Ibn al-Athir's *Usd al-ghaba*.

7.   Ibn Sa'd, *Al-Tabaqat al-kubra* (Beirut: Dar al-Fikr, 1980). Volume 8 is devoted to the subject of women. Ibn Sa'd lived in the 9th century. He died in A.H. 230. Ibn al-Athir, *Usd al-ghaba fi ma'rifat al-sahaba* (ed. Mustafa Wahbi, 1902). Volume 5 of this work is devoted to women. Ibn al-Athir died in A.H. 631 (13th century). Tabari, *Tarikh al-umam wa al-muluk*, op. cit. Tabari goes into the role of women at some length in a text inserted at the end of the thirteenth volume (Beirut: Dar al-Fikr, 1979). The author died in A.H. 310 (10th century). Ibn Hajar, al-'Asqalini, *Al-Isaba fi tamyiz al-sahaba* (biographies of the disciples of the Prophet), (Lebanon: Maktaba al-Muthanna, 1st ed., 1902). The author died A.H. 852 (15th century AD). Volume 7 is almost entirely devoted to women (pp. 224-506).

8.   Tabari, *Tafsir*, op. cit.

9.   She was born in A.H. 49 (AD 671) and died in the Spring of A.H. 117 (735 AD) in the reign of the tenth Umayyad caliph, Hisham Ibn 'Abd al-Malik, who came to power in January 724 AD.

10.   One of the most exciting biographies of Sakina is that by al-Isbahani, who speaks of her in several passages of the *Kitab al-aghani* (book of songs), Vol. 13, p. 361 et seq.; Vol. 16, p. 137 et seq.; Vol, 17, p. 159 and Vol. 19 p. 155 et seq. She is, however, mentioned in many works, particularly: Abi al-Hasan al-Maliqi, *Al-Hada'iq al-ghanna' fi akhbar al-nisa': tarajim shihirat al-nisa'*. This book first appeared in 1978

in Libya and Tunisia, edited by Dr Aida Tayyibi, who discovered the manuscript in the Chester Beatty Library in Dublin. The volume of Ibn 'Asakir's *Tarikh madinat Dimashq* (History of the city of Damascus), devoted to women, which was edited by Sakina Shahibi, contains a reference on p. 155. See also Zaynad Fawwaz al-'Amili, *Al-Durr an-manthur fi tabaqat rabbat al-khudur* (Bulaq, Egypt: Al-Matha'a al-Kubra, 1985); and 'Sakina' in *Dairat al-ma'arif al-Islamiyya*, Vol. 12, p. 19 et seq. Whole books have also been written on Sakina: See A'isha 'Abd al-Rahman, *Sakina Bint al-Hussein* (Beirut: Dar al-Kitab al 'Arabi, second edition, n.d.) – Ahmed 'Abd al-Halim, *Sakina Bint al-Hussein*, Cairo, 1969. N.B. This is not an exhaustive list. After A'isha, the wife of the Prophet, Sakina is probably the woman most written about by Muslim historians both male and female.

11.   *Kitab al-aghani*, Vol. 16, p. 143.

12.   Ibid., Vol. 11, p. 176 et seq. See also *Tarikh madinat Dimashq*, op. cit., p. 209; Abi al-Hasan al-Maliqi, *Al-Hada'iq*, op. cit., p. 55.

13.   Mu'awiya I, the founder of the Umayyad dynasty, came to power in year 41 of the *hijra* (661 AD) and was succeeded by Abu al-'Abbas al-Saffah, the first of the Abbasid caliphs.

14.   Al-Hadi, who came to power in AH 169 (AD 785), was the fourth Abbasid caliph. Al-Rashid was the fifth (170; AD 786), al-Ma'mun the seventh (198; AD 813) and al-Mutawakkil the tenth (232; AD 841).

15.   See *'jariya'* in Ibn Manzur, *Lisan al-'Arab* (Dar al-Ma'rifa, 1979 edition).

16.   Al-Jahiz, 'Kitab al-qiyan' in *Rasa'il* (Cairo, 1964).

17.   This passage from Al-Jahiz appears in a French translation by Charles Pellat as 'Les esclaves chanteuses', *Arabica*, Vol. 10, II, June 1963.

18.   Ibn Hazm al-Andalusi, 'Niqat al-'arus fi tawarikh al-khulafa' in *Al Rasa'il* (Collection of letters and short essays), ed. Hasan 'Abbas (Beirut: Al-Mu'assasat al-'Arabiyya li Dirasat wa Nashr, 1981, Vol. 2, p. 104. Ibn Hazm was born in 384 and died in 456.

19.   Abu al-Faraj al-Isbahani, *Al Ima' a Chawa' ir* (The slave-girl poets), edited by Dr Noury Mohammed al-Qaissi and Younes Ahmed as-Samarra'i, (Beirut: Maktabat al-Nahda al-'Arabiya, 1984); Al-Suyuti, *Al-Mustazraf min akhbar al-jawari*, annotated by Salah al-Din al-Munajid (Beirut: Dar al-Kitab al-Jadid, 1976). Al-Suyuti died in year A.H. 911 (1505 AD).

20.   On the *jawari* under the Abbasids, see Ahmad Amin, *Duha al-Islam* (Cairo: Maktabat al-Nahda al-Misriyya, 1961 (three volumes on social and cultural life, scientific movements and religious sects in the first Abbasid period). Ch. 4, 'Slavery and its cultural impact', provides a fine account of slavery under the Abbasids. On the *jawari*, and particularly the decline in the status of the free, aristocratic Arab woman as an effect of slavery, see Georgi Zaydan, *Tarikh at-tamaddun al-Islami* (History of Islamic civilization) (n.d.), 5 volumes, in 2 books. On slavery under the Abbasids, especially Vol. 4, p. 172 to Vol. 5, p. 27. On women under the Abbasid dynasty, see Vol. 5, p. 76 et seq. The best, brief overall account is that by the German orientalist, Adam Mez, in his *Die Renaissance des Islams*, Hildesheim, 1968 (rep. of 1st ed., Heidelberg, 1922).

21.   See below.

22.   Al-Jahiz, 'Les esclaves chanteuses'.

23.   Al-Isbahani, *Kitab al-aghani*, Vol. 16, pp. 343 et seq. The author died in A.H. 356 (AD 976).

CHAPTER IX

Women in Muslim History:
Traditional Perspectives
and New Strategies

Contrary to widespread belief, early Muslim historians gave considerable exposure to women in their writings. They did not, as might be expected, talk about them only as the mothers and daughters of powerful men. General history books, genealogies and chronicles identified women as active participants and fully involved partners in historical events, including the crucial emergence of Islam. In religious histories describing events which took place from the Prophet's birth to his death, as well as in religious texts themselves, such as Hadith repertories (testimonies of disciples concerning the Prophet's words and deeds) or Qur'an Tafsir (explanations, commentaries), women are acknowledged and their contribution generously praised as both disciples of the Prophet during his lifetime and as authors of Hadith after his death.

In fact, more than ever before, historical argument seems to be crucial to questions concerning the rights of women in Muslim theocracies. This is because all kinds of state policies to do with women, be they in the economic sphere (the right to work outside the home), or in the legal sphere (issues concerning personal status or family law), are justified and legitimized by reference to the tradition of the Prophet, that is, to historical tradition. Progressive persons of both sexes in the Muslim world know that the only weapon they can use to fight for human rights in general, and women's rights in particular, in those countries where religion is not separate from the state, is to base political claims on religious history.

A particularly illuminating debate taking place in the Muslim world today concerns whether or not there is a precedent for women to exercise political power in the highly controversial role of A'isha, the Prophet's third wife, who advised civil disobedience and herself led troops onto the battlefield in armed opposition to the fourth orthodox Caliph, 'Ali Ibn Abi Talib on 4 December AD 656 (A.H. 36), thereby contributing to his downfall. One of the results of the 'Ali–A'isha confrontation was the division of Muslims into Shi'a and Sunni, the Shi'a being unconditionally for 'Ali and, therefore, against A'isha as the symbol, among other things, of civil disobedience and of the right to contest the Caliph when he is believed to be in the wrong.[1] Even today, an outstanding Shiite ideologue, the Iranian 'Ali Shari'ati, holds that the ideal for Muslim women is Fatima, the Prophet's daughter, who played no noticeable political role in Islam.[2] A'isha is for the Shi'a the anti-model, the monstrous image of femininity. Women should content themselves, like Fatima, with being good mothers, daughters and housewives. In Egypt, Sa'id al-Afghani devoted ten years to writing his biography of A'isha. He says in his introduction and conclusion that he did so to show that women should be barred from politics. His book, *A'isha and Politics*, is a systematic marshalling of all conservative works on women to this end.[3]

The case of A'isha illustrates how closely the claim for or against women's rights is linked to historical scholarship in the Muslim world. Women's excellence in this field has had a tremendous impact. The definitive biography of A'isha by Zahiya Moustapha Khaddoura, a Lebanese woman scholar, which was written in the 1940s and republished in the 1970s, is a stunning rehabilitation of A'isha, which gives pride to Muslim women by supporting their claim, not only to political decision-making but also to legislation and *shari'a* (religious law) making.[4] A'isha produced more Hadiths (which are, besides the Koran, the revealed text, the source of the *shari'a*, the religious law) than 'Ali. According to Ibn Hajar, the author of the seventeen-volume *Fath al-Bari*, one of the most authoritative Hadith commentaries of *Boukhari Sahih* (authentic Hadiths, since thousands were frauds)[5] claimed that Caliph 'Ali contributed only 29 Hadiths, while A'isha contributed 242. And, since according to this widely acclaimed 15th century scholar (Ibn Hajar died in A.H. 852), *Boukhari sahih* do not total more than 1,602 Hadiths (and not as he previously believed 4,000), A'isha alone contributed more than 15 per cent of the bases of the *shari'a*.[6] Fatima, the daughter of the Prophet, upheld by Shi'a progressive ideologues like Shari'ati as the ideal for Muslim women today, did not contribute, although she was the Prophet's daughter; nor, according to the same source, did Caliph 'Ali's wife contribute more than one single Hadith.

Muslim historians have been forced to grant women their due in the volumes of traditional mainstream treatises. But they have also devoted a specific genre of work to women, a genre we can call (since they often used this title themselves) *Akhbar al-nisa* (Women's News). These are biographical portraits of famous individuals which are notable for their particular attention to detail and for their inclusion of themes that the methodological rules of scholarship prohibit in more mainstream work.

Salah ed-Din al-Munajid identified more than seventy such books in an article called 'What was Written on the Subject of Women',[7] which was an attempt to provide an exhaustive listing of every mention of these works by early historians. Of course, not all of them are available today due to destruction of libraries during foreign invasions, but many have been printed, and many more are still in manuscript form in Persian, Turkish and Arabic libraries (just to mention a few), waiting to come alive.[8]

The authors of these books were not dubious, unknown beginners. They included many of the most important scholars of both general and religious history as well as famous imams, literary figures and genealogists. The criteria for inclusion in these biographical portraits was the display of excellence in some field; beauty was just one of these criteria. Moreover, not only queens and aristocrats were included. Slaves made it into the 'Women's News' frequently and even managed on occasion totally to eclipse royalty and occupy primacy of place. A whole series of treatises on *Qiyan* – the cultural and literary contribution of women slaves to society – exists and begs thorough investigation.[9]

How then, with such a glowing presence in their history, do Muslim women come to have such a lowly image in their own society and in the world at large? In this chapter I try to answer that question and to challenge the situation.

As will be seen, the lowly image attributed to Muslim women in their own society today is not due to their absence from traditional memory or in written history. In fact, there is empirical evidence to show that the tradition of historicizing women as active, full participants in the making of culture (which we shall call *nisa'ist*, the Arabic synonym for feminist, from the word *nisa*, women) still continues today.[10] It could be said that the only novelty in this tradition is that women are now no longer simply objects of Muslim history. They have become subjects as well, they write history, side by side with men. They have, since the turn of the century, been actively involved in the writing of women's history.

The clue to this mystery resides partly in the fact that the image of women in society is not derived from historical material per se by any simple process, but is crucially dependent on the media which can either disseminate such research or restrict its dissemination. History, the recorded memory of a culture, is never consumed directly like other products. Historical material goes through highly complicated processes, often tightly controlled and censored by those in power, before it is presented to citizens for selectively orientated consumption. In order to simplify these multi-faceted, multi-connected processes, let us first make the basic assumption that possessing good historical material showing women as full participants in society is an advantage and can of course be recuperated and harnessed to a *nisa'ist* strategy.

Contrasting the wealth of historical evidence favourable to women with their lowly status in Muslim society leads to the inescapable conclusion that the forces shaping image-making in the Muslim world discriminate against them. But we should be careful to label these forces *conservative* and not *fundamentalist*, because, despite the way Western commentators frequently confuse the two, Muslim women's passivity in political, economic and cultural spheres cannot be explained by the influence of fundamentalism alone. In most Muslim countries fundamentalists are viewed with suspicion by those in power and considered politically undesirable by the state. This confusion between the terms conservative and fundamentalist does not further the understanding of a dynamic and complex situation.

While most Muslim regimes disagree politically with fundamentalists about almost everything, they do agree with them on women and their place in society. The very deep political conservatism at the basis of fundamentalist movements is mirrored in the political nature, opinions and aspirations of most Muslim regimes. If only fundamentalists are taken into account, it is impossible to understand why the disparaging, discrediting image of Muslim women is so present in national media and why discrimination against them attains the status of a sanctified act.

Medieval History and the Legitimization of Women's Rights

Medieval religious history is crucial for contemporary Muslim politics. As I mentioned earlier, those who make any kind of statement regarding the status of women are obliged to justify their pronouncements by citing precedents in religious history and tradition. State legislators, as well as fundamentalists, claim that their ideal model of the politically passive woman, barred from the public sphere and totally secluded and estranged from the society in which she lives, is derived from and legitimated by this history and tradition. A good example of this attitude is Mohammed Arafa's book, *Women's Rights in Islam*. He argues that women should not have political rights today because they never had them in the crucial period when the Prophet built the Muslim nation. The Prophet started to receive revelations in 610 when he was in his forties, emigrated to Medina in 622 (the first year of the Muslim calendar), created the first Muslim community there and died in 630. The years from 610 to 632 therefore constitute the reference, the model and the law. Mohammed Arafa states that 'during the first decades of

Islam, Muslim woman played no role whatsoever in public affairs, and this in spite of all the rights Islam bestowed on her, which are similar to those accorded to men. . . . Muslim history in its entirety ignores the participation of women, side by side with men, in the managing of the state affairs, at all levels'.[11]

There are many classical criteria for participation in the making of Islam. Among these, the individual must be identified as having been a disciple during the prophetic call period, while the Prophet was still alive. The person must have taken the oath of allegiance (*bay'a*) directly with the Prophet to fight for Islam's survival. And the individual must have contributed after the Prophet's death as an author of Hadiths, testimonies concerning the Prophet and his words and deeds. Using these criteria, Mohammed Arafa's thesis is difficult to support. Women are in fact identified as disciples in all the classical religious history books, which are the references and the source for Islam past and present. The following provides impressive evidence of this.

Historical sources

(a) In his famous directory of disciples' biographies, *Al-Isaba fi Tamyiizi al-Sahaba*, Shaikh Ibn Hajar (who died AH 852 of the Muslim calendar – AD 1474) acknowledges 1,552 women as disciples.[12] In a special section devoted to women (*Kitab al-nisa'*), which occupies a good part of Volume 5, he summarizes most of what has been written on the subject and is considered in Islam to be an important scientific author. He has been described both as the 'most outstanding of celebrities' (*Shaikh al-Islam*) and as the 'imam of the learned' (*Imam al-Huffad*). He is not, however, the first to have devoted an entire volume to female disciples' biographies, describing in minute detail their contribution during the first decades of Islam. The most famous of his predecessors is Ibn Sa'ad.

(b) Ibn Sa'ad's work on the 'great classes' (class meaning generation), *Al-Tabqat al-Kubra*, is an enormous compilation containing the events of the Prophet's life, as well as biographies of his chief companions. Volume 8, the last one, is devoted entirely to women. The importance of Ibn Sa'ad's work resides not only in its scientific rigour but also in the fact that it is among the oldest – he lived in the 9th century and died in the year 230 (AD 852). Since his death, other imams, in conformity with his approach (for example classifying the biographies in alphabetical order), have at various times tried to compile and complete the disciples' biographies and have never failed to give women their due prominence.

(c) Tabari (Abi Ja'far Mohammed Ibn Jarir), still one of the most quoted and referred to masters of religious history, could not resist ending the thirteenth volume of his history of nations and kings (*Tarikh al-umam wal-muluk*), in which women were already given wide coverage, by resummarizing the biographies of the disciples in what he called *al-Dayl* (long annexes, often books in themselves, this one having 115 pages).[13] Women are of course identified in many chapters as active participants and supporters of the Prophet in the making of early Islamic history. Tabari died in the year 310 (AD 932).

(d) Ibn Amir Yusuf-al-Namri al-Qurtubi, known as Ibn 'Abd al-Barr, who wrote his *Kitab al-Isti'ab* in the 11th century AD (he died in 463 AH), carried on the tradition and ended his multi-volume study with women's biographies. He is considered 'the crown of his peers' (*taju agranihi*). His text is presented, according to the printing tradition of religious literature, as a footnote in Ibn Hajar's *al-Isaba* and allows the Muslim reader to compare, at a glance on the same page, his 11th century biography with that of Ibn Hajar written four centuries later. Early Muslim religious scholars were masters in the special footnoting techniques of *hawamish* and *hawashi*, in which two (sometimes three) books on the same theme or event but from different centuries are printed on the same page. This allows researchers to check variations for each biography from one century to the other, thus making their own independent evaluations and drawing their own conclusions.[14]

(e) The 13th century (7th of the Muslim calendar) produced one more outstanding biographer of the disciples – Ibn al-Athir. He too did not forget women. He gave his disciples' biographies the title of *Usd al-ghaba* (literally 'The Forest Lions') and hundreds of women are identified and alphabetically classified among them in his 200-page book of women, *Kitab al-nisa'*.[15] He died in the year 631 (1253 AD).

(f) Al-Dahbi produced his own biographies of outstanding personalities among the nobles, *Siyar a'lam al-nubala*, in the 14th century. Here of course nobility was defined in its religious sense as the grace of having contributed to Islam's triumph. Women were classified among those who had that grace and all that accompanies it. Al-Dahbi died in 748 (AD 1370). This study of his, according to the editor of the most recent edition, is 'among the pride of Arab heritage'. One of the reasons for this is that it gives pre-eminence to the first decades of early prophetic Islam, while at the same time trying to cover all the ground from that time (7th century) to the author's own era (14th century).[16] Besides

general history and early religious history books, another historical genre yields incredibly detailed information on women and their position in society in early and even later Muslim centuries. This is the *nassab*, the genealogies. *Nassab* material is fascinating for contemporary researchers because it uncovers a wealth of information on particularly important topics – kinship patterns, marriage, divorce, conjugal life, sexual mores, childbirth and parenting, and women's initiatives in all these matters. The two following examples are selected only because they have been and are still considered achievements in the genre. Thorough listing and systematic investigation of this material is one of the tasks awaiting young generations of *nisa'ist* researchers.

(g) Abi Abdallah Ibn Mus'ab Al-Zubeiri's *Kitab Nassab Goraich* is definitely the most important and 'trusted proof' in Arab genealogy. It has two features which make it an especially precious document. First, it was written in the 9th century and is, therefore, one of the earliest of its kind and, second, the author 'puts a particular effort into tracing genealogies through women as well', according to Lery Provençal, who quoted edited and commented on its first publication.[17] This work has been widely quoted by all historians and biographers of disciples, including those mentioned above, such as Tabari and Ibn 'Abd-al-Barr, the author of *Kitab al-Isti'ab*.

(h) Ibn Hazm al-Andaloussi's *Jamharat ansab al-'Arab*, written a few centuries later in the 11th century (Ibn Hazm died in 152 AH) is notable because it both summarizes all the genealogical information accumulated until his time and also includes information on non-Arabs.[18] Berber, Persian and Jewish genealogies (he was an expert on the Torah) are also included. His study highlights links between Arabs and non-Arabs; women are present and visible and their sexual and reproductive life is documented like that of men.

(i) No study of religious history would be complete without mentioning the most quoted basic reference work for all Muslim historians, Ibn Hisham's biography of the Prophet, *Al-Sira al-Nabawiya*. Here the lives of women disciples appear to us tightly enmeshed in their historical context. They are depicted as actively involved in the Prophet's preaching, battles and debates.[19] Hisham's *Sira* is an epic fresco of the first decade of Islam's difficult birth (often overlooked today) and of each disciple's crucial contribution, support and detailed deeds. Here women appear as major builders of the faith. Without the emotional and intellectual support of Khadija, the Prophet's first wife, one wonders

what would have become of Islam in its particularly difficult beginnings in Mecca between 610 and 622. She was an influential and prosperous Mecca businesswoman, fifteen years his senior. She was knowledgeable about monotheism and thus convinced the Prophet, when he lived his first Qur'anic revelation experiences as terrifying events, that he was indeed the Prophet of a new God. According to the Prophet's own testimony in Hisham's *Sira*, it is to Khadija that he came, after his first encounter with Gabriel, the angel who contacted him on behalf of Allah in 610. He was then in his forties: 'I came back home and went to Khadija, and put my head on her thigh. She said, "Where were you, Father of Qassem?" [one of the Prophet's names, after one of their sons named Qassem] . . . I told her what happened [the visions and voices] and she said: "Good news, my cousin, and be assured by God. I want you to be this Nation's Prophet".'[20] Muhammad, explains Tabari, who quotes Hisham heavily, was afraid to be just a poet under the spell of his own creativity, as there were many who had such strong fits of inspiration.[21] Khadija was instrumental in convincing the troubled Prophet that his inspiration was indeed from divine origin and not simply a poetic and therefore human phenomenon. The interest of Hisham's *Sira* is that it is a fundamental text, and one of the earliest, most trusted and revered references for all later historians of the Muslim religion.

That women did not enter the battlefields simply to give first aid to the wounded, as we are repeatedly told in many contemporary conservative and fundamentalist writings, is amply confirmed in Ibn Hisham's description of one of the most disastrous battles the Prophet had to fight, the Battle of Ohod in March 625. A woman disciple who appears in all major religious history books, Nussaiba Bint Ka'b, describing her role during that battle, said that when she saw the Muslims were losing: 'I took position near the Prophet and I started fighting with my sword, in a defensive move around the Prophet. . . . I fought until I was wounded'.[22] It is no wonder then that contemporary *nisa'ist* intellectuals of both sexes have no difficulty proving, through the historical scholarship we shall identify in the strategy section, that women's passivity, seclusion and their marginal place in Muslim society has nothing to do with Muslim tradition and is, on the contrary, a contemporary ideological production.

Strategies for Enhancing the Image of Muslim Women

The best way to design effective strategies is to be pragmatic and start with what one has. As we have seen, as far as historical research on women *per se* is concerned, the Muslim world has almost everything. But what we lack is regional and international coordination of scarce skills, both in terms of communication between researchers and at the level where their findings can be fed to the various media for wider dissemination. There follow some specific proposals to improve the situation.

Producing historical research

Three themes, extremely important to all those involved in women's rights, could serve as the basis for three research projects. These are (1) research on the first decades of Islam and the production of biographies of outstanding Muslim women; (2) turn-of-the-century feminist research in Muslim countries; and (3) female slavery and prostitution in Islam. I will outline each of these in some detail to show the quality of the research potential on the one hand and the problems arising from the current lack of communication and coordination on the other.

The first decades of Islam

Any campaigner for women's rights is accused of importing Western models and ideas. The first decades of Islam, as we have seen, are very eloquent on women's contribution at that time and produce models of femininity like the active businesswoman Khadija, or the first *shari'a*-maker A'isha, the Prophet's third wife, or women who exercised political power within Muslim civilization. Data on women in the first decades of Islam are vital since conservative regimes and fundamentalists base their policies on women in Muslim tradition.

Sakina Shihabi's editing of the comments of Imam Ibn 'Asakir's special volume on women, *Tarikh Dimashq* (History of Damascus), is probably one of the best examples of this research [23] This text contains 196 biographies of famous Muslim women who either lived in or visited Damascus and it gave Ibn 'Asakir an opportunity to summarize all existing data until his time (12th century AD) on some of the most active and forceful women of our civilization. The volume on women is the last of an 80-volume history of Damascus, the editing of which Sakina Shihabi made her life's work. She carried out what is called in Arabic *tahqiq* (literally 'investigation') which means that she did extensive background research so that the modern reader could identify, by a simple glance at the reference at the bottom of the page, all names and events quoted. She explains her motives, since most of the rest of the volumes are still in manuscript form, for prioritizing the text on women: 'I preferred to bring alive Imam Ibn 'Asakir's volume on women . . . because it highlights a dimension of our Muslim civilization which is still totally obscure, that concerning women'.[24] She summarizes the importance of the work by saying that Ibn 'Asakir's women 'make vibrant five centuries of the political, social, literary and religious life of our civilization'.[25]

Having acknowledged the vital importance of this investigation, however, let us go on to look both at the difficulties she encountered in carrying out her work and the problems other scholars have in gaining access to her findings.

Sakina Shihabi illustrates some of the obstacles researchers face when she describes in the introduction to her book the difficulty she had in gaining access to the work of a colleague researching the same area, Dr Aida Tayyibi. The manuscript documents from which Shihabi was working were in a badly-damaged condition and, although Dr Tayyibi had published her edited edition of 'Ali al-Hassan al-Maliqi's classical 13th-century manuscript, *Biographies of Famous Women in Early Islam*, three years earlier, Shihabi was completely unable to acquire a copy of it or to link up with Tayyibi herself. In the end she had to obtain a copy of the original manuscript from the Chester Beatty Library in Dublin, Ireland. Here we have two researchers working on identical themes in the same language, yet, because they are isolated from one another and are short of funding, their efforts suffer from this appalling duplication of energy. Shihabi's own book is a bulky 678 pages, extremely expensive[26] and poorly distributed (no publisher is indicated).

Let us look, however, at some further research potential.

Omar Kahhala's *Most Outstanding Women in Both the Arab and Muslim World* is a bulky five-volume collection of biographies on women, particularly interesting for its scope (the Muslim world) and its time span. It includes early feminists such as the Lebanese, Turkish and Egyptian women who campaigned for human rights at the turn of the century, and describes their activities.[27] The author's introduction is dated 1959, which means that the book waited two decades to be published.

Zahiya Moustapha Khaddoura's already mentioned biography of *A'isha the Mother of Believers* is one of the best documents available on that most important model of femininity in Muslim history. The introduction to the first edition is dated 1947, but the book was only reprinted two decades later. It mentions that Dr Khaddoura presented it to obtain a diploma from the history department of Fouad First University.

Also important is Dr A'isha 'Abd al-Rahman's biography of *Sakina*

Bint al-Hussein, the little daughter of the Prophet who refused to veil and insisted on leading an active intellectual and political life. Dr 'Abd al-Rahman was working at Qaraouiyine University, Fez (Morocco) when the book was published.[28]

This list is merely an indication of the importance of the research that already exists in Arabic on women and does not pretend to provide an exhaustive or representative survey of the available data. Similar work has probably been carried out in Iranian and Turkish. A research project could identify systematically what has been done and where, and could evaluate whether texts are worth translating and publishing and, if so, what needs to be done to make this possible. The researchers identified above could easily be traced through their publishers. Setting up networks for coordination between *nisa'ist* history researchers and activists and linking these to feminist publishers and the media could help bring together all the scattered energy already at work both inside and outside the Muslim world.

Feminist research at the turn of the century

Many Western feminists were surprised by Margot Badran's biography of the Egyptian feminist, Huda Sha'arawi (1879-1924), for they had been convinced that Muslim women were no more than obsequious followers in the struggle for women's rights.[29] It is true, though, that even in the Muslim world, this turn-of-the-century feminist movement had been totally forgotten, its memory swept aside by the wave of conservative and fundamentalist opinion into which the media had sunk. This is one reason why it has become necessary to organize a workshop to carry out systematic investigations into what has been written and to make suggestions about how best to ensure that it becomes more accessible. The following examples give an idea of the rich accumulation of data which are already available but scattered throughout the Muslim world.

A Turkish author, Dr Bahriye Uçok, has researched and produced some valuable biographies of women who exercised political power in Muslim countries. Such data are crucial for today's debates with fundamentalists and conservatives, who state that women have no political role. *Al-Nisa' al-hakimat fi al-tarikh* (Women who exercised political power in History) is a well-researched document on some of the women who took over political power in such far-flung corners of the Muslim world as Persia, Egypt, India, Muslim Spain and the Maldive Islands.[30] Although the book was translated into Arabic and published in 1973, it is out of print and available only from libraries. This is a pity, since it is trim, concise (173 pages), well written and easily accessible even to a high-school readership. Translation of such books into Iranian,

Urdu, Swahili, Malaysian, Indonesian and other Muslim languages would be useful, and publication in a cheap, well-distributed series would maximize their impact.

All this early feminist research on women in various parts of the Muslim world needs to be checked out, translated and given adequate media coverage. Attention should also be paid to nationalist movements in the Muslim world because nationalists have debated the question of women's status and rights in their attempts to try to understand why Muslim societies were defeated by Western powers. But our knowledge of this subject has come mainly from men and women's contribution remains largely unknown.

There are, however, some important clues. For example, in the 1890s Zaynab Fawwaz al-'Amili, an Egyptian woman writer, published a 552-page compilation of women's biographies called *Generalizations of Secluded Housewives* (*Al-Durr al-manthour fi tabaqat rabbat al-khodour*). In her introduction she says that she undertook the work 'to contribute to her sex's enhancement, and because that is the best gift one can give women'.[31] This indicates that, not only was women's historical research being undertaken at that time, but there was also a significant demand for it. The writer states that she herself was secluded and that this greatly impeded her investigations. Freedom of movement to pursue research was one of the goals she wished to achieve. Another example is that of the Turkish author, Princess Qladriya Husseyn, who wrote a volume called *The Most Famous Women in the Moslem World* (*Shihhirat nisa' fi l'alam al-Islami*), although in this case the style was closer to that of a novel than to academic research.[32]

It is evident from these and other examples that women's historical research in Islam experienced an important moment at the end of the 19th and beginning of the 20th centuries. These researchers were women who both analysed their own situation in the contemporary Muslim world and contested it on historical grounds. But who were they? In which countries did the movement start? What was its significance? Where is the material it produced and how can it be used today?

A systematic regional survey, mapping feminist historical research in the Muslim world between the late 1890s and the Second World War, could establish what data exist in at least some of the major Islamic languages – Indonesian, Arabic, Urdu, Turkish and Iranian, for example. Such a survey could cover already published material, as well as give some indication of what manuscripts were available and in what languages, so that these could be fed into further strategies for translation and coordinated, perhaps initially in Turkey, Iran, the Arab states and in Urdu and Swahili-speaking countries.

Female slavery and prostitution in Islam

There are important data on this theme, which are usually scattered throughout the various multi-volumed studies already mentioned, especially those of Tabari, Ibn 'Asakir, and Hisham's *Sira*. Clarifying Islam's position on slavery and prostitution and establishing how it has continually been violated, could strengthen women's position. Women campaigning for their rights might find here the arguments with which to invalidate conservative and fundamentalist grounds for interpreting the *shari'a*. One document of this kind may be mentioned briefly. In the 12th century, that is five centuries after the Qur'an made a strong stand against slavery, Ibn Batalan wrote a treatise giving rich men advice on how to buy slaves, including information on how to test women for physical fitness, according, of course, to whether they were to be used for work or sexual pleasure [33] Since slavery and prostitution go hand in hand, searching out and exposing this material will highlight the fact that the degradation of women in Muslim countries is a violation of the Qur'an and its principles and laws. Serious historical research could, through a study of the past, help to lift the veil on this taboo topic in today's societies, where a careful silence surrounds prostitution and its clients.

Dissemination strategies

Women can learn something from the effective way in which fundamentalists use the media to disseminate information throughout Islam. Everyone has heard about fundamentalist literature on women, but very rarely are people exposed to *nisa'ist* research. This is because the fundamentalists have a comprehensive regional and international strategy, involving rapid translation into the main Islamic (Turkish, Iranian, Arabic, Urdu) and Western (English, French) languages, as well as well-organized distribution and dissemination of printed material around the world at affordable prices. If one never hears about *nisa'ist* research, which has produced first-class scholarship on Muslim women, it is because it is being produced by isolated researchers working in difficult conditions and because it has failed to find its way into the media. Moreover, much of it is expressed in rather heavy academic jargon, exists in only one of the many Islamic languages, and is often published in obscure collections, which are more often than not out of print. There are now many Muslim women trying to set up publishing houses and make films to convey different images of women. Creating links between researchers on the one hand and media skills on the other would, in itself, encourage more research and maximize its impact on society. Another vital link is between professional historians and feminist activists in need of their research findings.

Research is, by definition, an unfinished product. Producing historical data on women is just one part of the process. Feeding the research findings into the channels that need them and are likely to make good use of them is another. The problem is essentially one of coordination and the setting up of networks. Regional and international links would allow the findings of isolated researchers to flow to all those who need them and thus encourage both more research and better use of it.

Nisa'ist publishing initiatives

Nisa'ist publishing is thriving despite all kinds of material and political difficulties. With more financial backing, however, not only would publishers be encouraged to work together and coordinate their efforts, but they would be able to launch a more coherent publishing strategy throughout the Muslim world.[34]

Special mention should be made of the presence in the West of numerous women scholars from Islamic societies, who have often preferred to live abroad to preserve their creativity and who play a particularly important role in publishing historical research or in coordination networks, translation teams, publishing and other media activities on the Western intellectual stage. The AMEWS (Association for Middle-East Women's Studies) would be in a position to mobilize researchers interested in Muslim women's history.

Finally, a rapid translation committee needs to be set up, not only to give information about research that has been written in other languages, but also to cater for those who do not speak Arabic (the language of textual revelations and of primary scholarship on Islam) and to produce continually updated lists of new publications in Arabic to enable Urdu, Indian, Turkish and Indonesian researchers and publishers to plan for the future translation and publication of relevant material.

A sub-committee translating pertinent data on women's religious history from Arabic into English should also be set up. Since many Arab researchers are operating from Western universities, they could play a key role in translating both information and documents into English. The AMEWS is sufficiently skilled to do this. It is well known now that if an Arabic study is translated into English it becomes more accessible to other Muslim researchers working in, say, Urdu or Iranian. Translations from one Islamic language into another are more easily carried out if there already exists an English translation of the original, for it is easier to find translators from, for example, English into Urdu than from Arabic into Urdu. Identifying scholars able to translate from Arabic into English would therefore improve communications between researchers throughout the Arab region and at the same time render the data accessible to Western readers.

Notes

1.   For two concise résumés of the historical background and complex reasons for the split between Shi'a and Sunni, see Henri Corbin, 'Le Schisme et la philosophie prophétique', in *Histoire de la philosophie Islamique* (Paris: Gallimard, 1986) and Mohammed Abu Zahre, 'Furuq al-medhab al-Shi'-i, in *Al-Madshib al-Islamiya'* (Egypt: Maktabat al Adhab, n.d.).

2.   For an analysis of Shariati work and its impact on women's rights in Iran, see Adèle K. Ferdow, 'Women and the Islamic Revolution', *International Journal of Middle East Studies* 15 (1983), pp. 283-98. The references to Fatima as a model are on pp. 288 ff.

3.   Sa'id al-Afghani, *A'isha wa-al-Siyasse*, (Beirut: Dar al-Fikr, 1971).

4.   Zahiya Moustapha Khaddoura, *A'isha the mother of Believers*, (Beirut: Dar al-Kitab al-Arabi, 1972). The introduction is dated 1943.

5.   Fatima Mernissi, 'Le Prophet et les Hadithe' and 'Enquête sur un Hadith misogyne et sur son auteur Abu Bakre', in *Le Harem Politique* (Paris: Michel Albin, 1987, chs. 2 and 3. A summary of these findings was presented to the Georgetown University Eleventh Avenue Symposium on 'Women in Arab Society, Old Boundaries, New Frontiers', 10-11 April 1986.

6.   Ibn Hajar, 'Asqlani al-sari moqaddimat', *Fath al-bari*, Vol. 1 (Egypt: a-Matb'a al-Mostapha al-Halabi, 1962), pp. 247 ff.

7.   Salah al-Din al-Mounajid, 'Ma ullifa ani al-nisa' majallat majma', *Lugha al-arabiya* 16 (1941), p. 216.

8.   Since 1941 several of the books which were still in manuscript form have been printed, thanks to the efforts of pro-women scholars such as Salah al-Din al-Mounajid.

9.   A sample of this genre is Abu al-Faraj al-Isbahani's *Slave Women Poets* (al-Ima' a-Shawa'ir) in the 10th century; see also Abu al-Faraj al-Isbahani, *Al-Ima a-Shawa'ir*, ed. Noury Mohammed al-Qaissi and Younes Ahmed al-Samarrai (Beirut: Maktabat al-Nahda al al-'Arabiya, 1984.)

10.   The equivalent of the word feminism in Arabic is coined from the word *nisa'* (women). Many compositions with this word as a radical have been adopted to express feminist ideas or claims in many Arab conferences, including one organized in Cairo by Nawal Saadawi, president of the Arab Women's Solidarity Association, in September 1986. But, as always happens, and this is natural in democratic contexts, each political faction tries to add a consonant here or a vowel there to give the word *nisa'* its ideological connotation: *niswani, nisa'i, nusswanati*. I find the word *nisa'* by itself so charged with energy that for me, it means a whole programme of self-liberation just by itself. I would not therefore add anything to it but the adjectival ending which consists of adding a simple 'i' to *nisa*, whence *nisa'i*. *Nisa'i* is for me an adjective that designates any idea, project, programme, or hope that supports women's rights to full-fledged participation in and contribution to remaking, changing and transforming society, as well as full realization of one's own talents, needs, potentials, dreams and virtualities. And it is in this sense that I have always lived and defined women's liberation, whatever the language –

'feminism' or *nisa'ism*. In this chapter, however, since I am describing the dynamics and the debate around women and history in the Muslim world, I use the Arabic word *nisa'ist* to identify the progressive current supporting women's rights through historical scholarship, since Arabic is the only Islamic language I know, and also because most of the historical documents to which I shall be referring are in Arabic, although their authors may be Iranians, or Turks, etc. This progressive *nisa'ist* feminist current includes men as well as women. The content of the historical work, the ideological target of the conclusions, are taken into account, not the sex of the author.

11.   Mohammed Arafa, *Huquq al-mar'a fil-Islam*, 3rd edn. (Place of publication not indicated, Al-Maktab al-Islami, 1980), p. 149.

12.   Sheikh Ibn Hajar, *Al-Isaba fi tamyiizi al-sahaba* (Lebanon: Maktabat al-Mouthanna, 1902).

13.   Tabari, 'Al-Mountakhab min Kitab al-dayl al-moudayyal min tarikh al-sahaba wal-tabi'in', *Tarikh al-umam wa-l-muluk*, Vol. XIII (Beirut: Dar al-Fikr, 1979).

14.   Ibn 'Abd-al Barr's *Kitab al-Isti'ab* appears in Appendix II of Ibn Hajar's *al-Isaba*.

15.   Ibn al-Athir, 'Usd al-ghaba fi ma'rifat al-sahaba' in al-Matba's *al-Wahbiya*, ed. and compiled by Moustapha Wahbi, Vol. V, 1920. *Kitab al-nisa'* runs from pp. 389 to 642.

16.   Al-Dahbi, *Siyar a'lam al-Mubala* (Cairo: Dar al-ma'arif, 1958), p. 38. See especially Vol. II, in which a concentration of women's biographies is listed.

17.   Abi 'Abdallah bnu Mus'ab al-Zubeiri, *Kitab nassab goruich* (Cairo: Dar al-Ma'arif), 1950. The quotation is from Lery Provençal's introduction, p. 9.

18.   Ibn Hazm al-Andaloussi, *Jamharat ansab al-'Arab* (Cairo: Dar al-Ma'arif, n.d.).

19.   Ibn Hisham, *Al-Sira al-Nabawiya*, Beirut, Dar Ihys al-Thurat al-Arabi, n.d.

20.   Hisham, *Sira*, Vol. I, p. 254.

21.   Tabari, *Tarikh*, Vol. II, p. 208.

22.   Hisham, *Sira*, Vol. III, pp. 86, 87.

23.   Imam Ibn 'Asakir, *Tarikh Dimashq* (Damascus: 1982). Special volume on women edited by Sakina Shihabi.

24.   'Asakir, *Tarikh Dimashq*, p. 5.

25.   'Asakir, *Tarikh Dimashq*, p. 33.

26.   It costs 160DH, the equivalent of 200 francs or roughly 40 US dollars, which relative to purchasing power is a prohibitive price.

27.   Omar Kahhala, *Most Outstanding Women in Both the Arab and Muslim World* (Damascus: Mu'assassat al-Rissala, 1982).

28.   Ai'sha 'Abd al-Rahman, *Sakina Bint al-Hussein* (Beirut: Dar al-Kitab al-'Arabi, n.d.).

29.   Margot Badran, *Harem Years: the Memoirs of an Egyptian Feminist* (London: Virago, 1986).

30.   Bahriye Uçok, *Al Nisa al-hakimat fi al-tarikh*, trans. into Arabic by Ibrahim Daqouq (Baghdad: Matba'a al-Sa'doun, 1973).

31.   Zaynab Fawwaz al-'Amili, *Al-Durr al-manthour fi tabaqat rabbat al-khodour* (Boulaq, Egypt: al-Matba'a al-Kubra, 1982, 1985).

32.   Princess Qadriya Husseyn, *Shihhirat nisa' fi 'alam al-Islami*, trans. into Arabic by 'Abd al-'Aziz Amin al-Khanji (Egypt: Husseyn Husseyn Publications, 1924).

33.   Ibn Batalan, Risala fi shariy al-raqiq (Cairo: Dar al-Fikr al Arabi, 1954).

34.   There are already *nisa'ist* groups publishing research or translations in Pakistan (Simrog Women's Resource and Publication Centre, Lahore), France (The Arab Women's Solidarity Association, Doreya al-Awn, Paris), Morocco (Editions le Fennec, Casablanca), the United States (AMEWS, Association for Middle East Women's Studies, University of California, Davis, Ca. 95616).

CHAPTER X

Femininity as Subversion: Reflections on the Muslim Concept of *Nushuz*

Nushuz is a Qur'anic concept; it means the rebellion of the wife against her Muslim husband's authority. The Qur'an only refers to *nushuz* in order to describe the punishment a husband must inflict upon the wife in case she rebels., Ghazali defines the *nashiz* (the woman who rebels) as a wife who confronts her husband either in act or word. He explains that the word *nashz* means 'that which tries to elevate itself above ground.'[1]

I do not want here to elaborate a theory of the concept of surrender in Islamic thought. Fatna Sabbah has done that convincingly in *The Woman in the Muslim Unconscious* (1984). She argues, and I agree with her, 'that the ideal of female beauty in Islam is obedience, silence and immobility, that is inertia and passivity. These are far from being trivial characteristics, nor are they limited to women. In fact, these three attributes of female beauty are the three qualities of the believer vis-à-vis his God. The believer must dedicate his life to obeying and worshipping God and abiding by his will.'[2] Fatna Sabbah explains that the woman's obedience to the husband is not just a marginal device in Islam; she demonstrates that it is a central element and a key law for the viability of the system. 'In the sacred universe,' she states, after having analysed the orthodox Sunni Islamic discourse, 'the believer is fashioned in the image of woman, deprived of speech and will and committed to obedience to another (God). The female condition and the male condition are not different in the end to which they are directed, but in the pole around which they orbit. The lives of beings of the male sex revolve around the divine will. The lives of beings of the female sex revolve around the will of believers of the male sex. And in both cases the human element, in terms of multiple, unforeseeable potentialities, must be liquidated in order to bring about the triumph of the sacred, the triumph of the divine, the non-human.'[3]

I want to suggest that women's disobedience is so feared in the Muslim world because its implications are so enormous. They refer to the most dreaded danger to Islam as a group psychology: individualism.

Muslim societies resist women's claim to changing their status, and they repress feminist trends which are actually evident all over the Muslim world, condemning them as Western imports, not simply because these societies fear women, but because they fear individualism.

Individualism, the person's claim to have legitimate interests, views and opinions different from those of the group, is an alien concept and fatal to heavily collectivist Islam. Islam, like any theocracy, is group-orientated, and individual wishes are put down as impious, whimsical, egotistical passions. I would suggest, however, that the woman, identified in the Muslim order as the embodiment of uncontrolled desires and undisciplined passions, is precisely the symbol of heavily suppressed individualistic trends. I believe that if the issues of the veil and of women's rights are so central to Muslim fundamentalist movements today, it is because these movements can be interpreted as strong visceral reactions against individualism. The primary issue being debated in the Muslim world today is democracy – the individual right to choose society's rulers. The right of each citizen to choose those who rule, through clear voting procedures, is a total reversal of the idea of personhood in Islam. It is the world upside-down. Democracy indicates clearly that it is the individual who is the sacred source of political authority, and not the group. Islam, like all theocracies, puts the emphasis on the *umma* as a mythically homogeneous group, which is the legitimate source of authority. The objective of Muslim society is the survival of the *umma*, not the happiness of the individual. The latter is totally submissive to the religious law which binds his/her acts and thought in all spheres of human experience, from the most public to the most intimate.

In these few pages I want to indicate that we will not understand the resistance of Muslim societies to the change in women's status and rights if we do not take into account the symbolic function of women as the embodiment of dangerous individualism. It is this individualism that society has chosen to repress in order to safeguard a collective orientation. Therefore I will discuss the notion of *nushuz* (rebellion or subversion) as it is linked to one of the most individualistic concepts of Islam, the concept of *bid'a*, that is, innovation; we will then look at women's rebellion through the historical profiles of dissenting women; and finally, we will see the implications of women's dissent in the present situation, namely in the integral relatedness of three phenomena: women's claim to change, the disintegration of traditional society, and the invasion of Western, capitalist, consumerist individualism. In this last part, I want to clarify why most feminists in the Muslim world are faced with the threat of being labelled as Western agents, traitors or enemies

of the community. The Western hedonist and consumerist invasion of
Muslim societies is, of course, seen as a disruption of the social fabric,
and women who claim change – and therefore claim their own
individuality – are viewed as agents of such disruption.

Individualism as a Crime Against the Sacred Law: The Concept of *Bid'a* and Its Proximity to the Concept of *Nushuz*

Bid'a is 'innovation'. It is the capacity of the individual to change his or
her fate, life and thoughts about people and things, and to act critically
in accordance with one's own assessment of the situation. *Bid'a* is
considered as a deadly sin in Islamic orthodoxy. *Bid'a* is not only error,
it is a crime, in that one steps out of the 'right path' traced out and
organized by the sacred law of the group. It is deviating from the straight
path, the *tariq al-mustaqim*, and is dangerous not only because innovators
dissent from the community, but because in doing so they challenge the
very existence of order based on consensus. In Islamic cosmogony, the
sexes play an important role in symbolizing obedience and authority.
One sex can be the masters of women and the slaves of God, and that
is the male sex; the other can be slaves only, and that is the female sex.
In no way can women take the initiative. If they do, the whole order is
in jeopardy, since their function and duty is to obey.

It is of real significance that Arabic has a special word for women's
rebellion – *nushuz*. What happens, then, when *nushuz* occurs? What
happens when women rebel and seize their own authority, refuse to
obey the sacred laws in a theocracy? Did this ever happen? And if it did
what was society's response? It was strong and immediate. Why? As we
shall see, the resistance to women's rebellion does not concern women
alone – it concerns men as well. If the women, the embodiment of duty,
rebel, then what about the men who have the double role of master and
slave? They are likely to be faced with the fact that their 'slaves' rebel
'better' than they do, and that their 'slaves' exercise power and take the
initiative. This, as one can imagine, undermines the whole hierarchical
order.

I want to suggest through several examples that the notion of equality
between men and women is profoundly threatening to the Muslim
hierarchical order. The notion of a strong bond between a man and a
woman, expressed in English by the word 'couple', does not exist in
Arabic. Arabic has fifty words for 'love', but no word for 'couple'.[4] This
linguistic lapse, far from being a random event, is as I see it a crystal-
clear symbolic message in societies where rigid sex-role stereotyping is

so fundamental to hierarchical order, that when women challenge the status quo they threaten not only patriarchal power (their relation to the husband), but the very existence of the entire system (and more specifically God's claim to obedience). The inflation of words for love is, in my view, a mystification, an attempt to hide the absence of the couple in the Muslim family, which is made institutionally unstable by the practices of repudiation and polygamy.

In recent years, the threat of *nushuz*, women's rebellion, has been activated in Islam by the rise of women's consciousness regarding gender issues and by writings about women's liberation in the Muslim world. It is rooted, however, in the fears the *umma*, the Muslim community, has had for many centuries: the fear of dissent. The fear of the individual standing up to claim his or her private interests as a legitimate source of social organization; the fear of change and innovation; the fear of division and dispersion within Islam; the fear of atomization of the centuries-old myth of group solidarity and collective spirit. The struggle of the Muslim community to maintain the myth of unity came from centuries of fighting heterogeneity and dissent, starting with the huge still-unsolved problem of who should head that community. The authoritarian tradition of Islam came precisely from its expansion, its success in very different lands and cultures in Asia, Africa and Europe – all of which strengthened the authoritarian claim for unity. A claim which imperialistic interest nurtured precisely because dissent, from the start, was tearing that community apart.

In the 1990s, the fear within the *umma* is stronger than ever before, because there are threats to consensus not only from without (the West as a deadly enemy with an invading culture), but from within as well. The increasing access of the poor to education, the incredibly high social mobility, the polarization of classes around economic issues, the emergence of women as salaried workers – all these pose a threat to the Muslim community as it traditionally viewed itself, a homogeneous group.

Submission, in the Muslim tradition, has also come to include submission to God's interpreters here on earth: caliphs, imams and their empowered staff in private spheres, i.e. husbands. In the Islamic vision of human society based upon submission or surrender to God, authority flows from the top to the bottom. Every individual is integrated into a flawless order, with duties and rights clearly defined. A strong sense of belonging stems from integration into this pyramidal order, in which roles and ways of conduct are minutely defined according to age, sex and access to wealth and knowledge.

Access to knowledge is not a human right but a privilege bestowed by God upon believers. It is thus a key factor in the ordering of society. Islam is the religion of knowledge. Intelligence (*aql*) is an instrument of knowing God; with it one penetrates the meaning of the 'signs' (*ayat*) which only the elect can decode. In Islam there is no conflict between God and scientific inquiry, for the decoding of the signs of the universe expands our knowledge of God's might and his bewildering creation. But not all Muslims as individuals are equal in their ability to decode the signs of God, to know God, and to transcend sense and gross material involvement. Hence the necessity to rely on the group.

Submission, obedience to divine law, is for both sexes and is the duty of every Muslim who wants to strengthen the *umma*. Islam, submission, means to acknowledge the authority of the laws, not to make them. Making the law is the unique privilege of God. God makes his will known through his prophets and through signs available in our surroundings: the prophets' task is precisely to help make them accessible. There is no clergy in Islam as we are repeatedly told, but that does not mean that there is no male hierarchy controlling the understanding of the Qur'an's meaning. These are the élite male interpreters of the sacred laws, and when we are debating, for example, the veil issue, we are not debating how women feel about it, but what Abu so-and-so or Bukhari said, we are debating which male authority's opinion is the prevailing one. Not what women are feeling or desiring.

Sakina and A'isha: Feminists of the First Century of Islam

The ideal model of femininity upheld by orthodox Sunni Islam is that of an obedient woman, one who is physically modest. Such a woman does not challenge laws and orders. She veils her body and keeps it available for the husband only. Veiling goes together with a key attribute, modesty, and is the expression of the spatial confinement of women. Spatial confinement is the physical expression of women's exclusion from the public sphere, the precise sphere of knowledge and power. This explains why Muslim conservative activists, manipulating Islam as a disciplinary framework for their claim to guide and decide for their supporters, will insist on women's modesty. Female modesty has a wider symbolic function: it refers to the need for the believer to curb his initiative and critical judgement.

Muslim history, from the first century to the present, has had to struggle with women's refusal to conform to such models. Each century had to find a response to *nushuz*, from the time of Sakina, the 7th century rebel (1st Muslim century), to present-day rebels, such as those in Egypt,

Algeria, Morocco and elsewhere. Women always struggled against the passive models of femininity but they never were as threatening as they are now, because women's dissent expresses itself through writing. Before, women's resistance to patriarchy was not recorded, it was oral, it confined itself to tales, proverbs or acts. A look at several instances of *nushuz* across the centuries will give us a sense of the continuing threat women rebels pose to the public realm.

Sakina's Rebellion: The First Century

Starting with the first century, qadis and imams seem to have faced the refusal of some women to accept the Muslim laws related to veiling, seclusion, polygamy and obedience to the husband. These women refused to veil, and insisted on the right to go about freely without asking the husband's permission. They insisted on keeping the right to entertain relations with men other than their husbands, often poets with whom they could engage in intellectual exchange outside the house.

These women also refused the basic principle of Muslim marriage: the husband's authority over the wife and his right to polygamy and repudiation. They insisted on putting conditions which preserved their freedom into the marriage act, and deprived the husband of the right to change residence at will, to have many wives, or to divorce by repudiation. They therefore secured for themselves the right Islam denies a woman: the right to leave her husband when she pleases.

Muslim theologians could not prevent this first wave of women 'feminists' from subverting the law because they had three assets which gave them incredible power over the qadis and caliphs in charge of enforcing law and order. The three assets were beauty, intelligence and aristocracy. This combination was enough to justify a woman's claim to *nushuz*-rebellion against the prevailing models of femininity.

The conditions Sakina put in her marriage act with one of her husbands, Zayd, made of her a celebrity and a *nashiz*, a rebellious wife. She stipulated that he would have no right to another wife, that he could never prevent her from acting according to her own will, that he would let her elect to live near her woman friend, Ummu Manshuz, and that he would never try to go against her desires (*Agani XIV*, pp. 168, 169. Mada'ini, *Kitab al-muraddafat*, p. 66). When the husband once decided to go against Sakina's will and went one weekend to his concubines, she took him to court, and in front of the Medina judge she shouted at him, 'Look as much as you can at me today, because you will never see me again!' (*Agani* XVI, p. 155.)

Sakina was described by al-Zubairi, a historian who, like many others, was full of admiration for her, in these words: 'She radiates like an ardent fire. Sakina was a delicate beauty, never veiled, who attended the Quraish Nobility Council. Poets gathered in her house. She was refined [*zarifa*] and playful.'[6]

Sakina, extravagantly elegant, set the tone of fashion in the then economically thriving Hijaz, Arabia Felix, where happiness and the good life were possible thanks to Islam's conquering power. The power of the Muslim empire had shifted by then from Mecca to the north, to Syria and Iraq. Rich Quraish families whose wealth had been enhanced by the triumph of Islam lived lavishly and peacefully in the increasingly politically marginal Arabia. One example of this lavish, relaxed and hedonistic Arabian life is that not only did women copy Sakina's hairdo, but men did too! The pious Caliph 'Umar ibn 'Abd al-'Aziz felt, in time, the need to intervene and ordered his 'police' to punish and shave the heads of those men who insisted on adopting Sakina's hairstyle.

Another *nashiz* of this century was A'isha Bint Talha, the daughter of Caliph Abu Bakr through her mother. She refused to veil, and when asked why said, 'God the mighty distinguished me by my beauty. I want people to see that, and acknowledge my superiority over them. I will not veil. No one can force me to do anything.' (*Agani* XI, p. 176.)

These *nashiz* who defied openly the Muslim model of female modesty and obedience were, because of their social rank, very prominent women and were, therefore, a threat to the pattern of religious authority. The theologians decided to fight back and to put a stop to *nushuz*. In law, *nushuz* is addressed as a social problem. For example, al-Muwatta (II, p. 6) states that a man has the right to take his wife where he wishes, regardless of what *nashiz* women put in their marriage contracts. Another example in al-Muwatta (II, p. 14) tries to discourage *nushuz* by stating that the husband is not bound by marriage contract conditions depriving him of his right to polygamy.

Feminism as an Internal Threat to Muslim Order: Implications of *Nushuz*

Although women have had access to education only in the last few decades, they have gained an incredibly high visibility in the public sphere. In most Arab countries, for example, a quarter of university teachers are women. Although women are barred from important political posts, they have gained substantial access to middle-level positions in national administrations and do strive to get a more and more important share of the salaries distributed in both private and public sectors.

Moreover, they have now started to use writing to express their desire for changing their status and the society around them. In 1983 a feminist magazine appeared in Arabic in Morocco: *The Eighth of March* sold 20,000 copies within the first few months. The year 1985 witnessed the publication of another 'popular' magazine in Tunisia called *Nisa'* (women). These examples are perceived as extremely dangerous by many conservatives, since they do not try to proselytize among elites or in university settings, but recruit readers from among lay persons. Feminism is no longer limited to a few women's salon-like discussions; it has become identified by many women as the ground for voicing economic and political discontent which is impossible to push through trade unions and political parties. Let me simply cite three instances of women's rebellion in the present century, primarily to give a sense of the ways in which *nushuz* continues to be a threat in the Muslim world.

The first was in Algeria during the Revolution. The renowned historian Harbi, an important political figure of revolutionary Algeria, in exile since 1973, gave an interview in *Révoltes logiques* called 'Women in the Algerian Revolution'. It is perhaps the most discrediting documented statement on the ambiguities and hesitations of the Algerian revolution when it comes to the issue of women in relation to equality and democracy. Harbi explains that the revolutionary 'brothers' were totally traditional in their contacts and encounters with women in the Maquis, the guerilla camps. They did everything they could to prevent women from escaping traditional roles; they used women for both traditional needs, such as sex and cooking, and modern needs, such as logistics and carrying arms.

This I mention in order to explain that one of the most important modern revolutions the 20th century has witnessed, the Algerian revolution, showed that Arab society, even as it was forced to make many sacrifices and to adopt radical change, resisted violently the idea of sacrificing sexual inequality. Algerian revolutionaries hoped to keep women in their proper place, even as they fought for radical change in almost everything else. A second example is from Tunisia. In March 1983, the monthly journal for 'democracy and socialism', *L'Avenir*, one of the voices of opposition to Bourguiba, published an interview with a Muslim feminist, entitled 'I am a Rebel'. Only those who knew the story behind that title could appreciate the challenge it posed. The Muslim woman interviewed was Nawal el Saadawi, the Egyptian writer, doctor and feminist. President Bourguiba, who listened to the interview on television, was furious when he realized that she never mentioned his name when talking about liberation movements among Arab women. He then gave orders to dismiss the person responsible in Tunisian television, since he had allowed an Arab woman to talk about liberation without mentioning Bourguiba, the Great Warrior (al-Mujahid al-akbar).

For Bourguiba, a man who is one of the most advanced on the women's question, women's liberation is a man's affair. And it is true that, until the last three decades, the liberation of women was a man's prerogative. The Arab woman, according to modern Islamic thought, is a simple instrument: she will obey when told to liberate herself according to orders. For *L'Avenir* to repeat that Nawal proclaims herself a rebel is to tell Bourguiba that women rebel, sometimes even without being told to do so!

The third example is from March 1983 in Rabat. In the crowded room of the Human Rights Association, Rue Soussa, which is also the Headquarters of the Moroccan Branch of the Arab Writers' Federation, two hundred people gathered. The group became sharply divided when a number of women, most of them wives of political prisoners, started to talk about their experiences as women in an authoritarian state. They began to analyse their own daily struggle with their husbands, with the prison administration, and with the justice ministry. But all said that these latter struggles were minor compared to those with their own 'revolutionary' husbands: the struggle to get their own men to rise higher than the prerogatives of husbands and the privileges of patriarchy to become real persons in relation to their militant wives. To be a political militant, they said, does not automatically liberate a man from oppressive attitudes and reactions toward his wife.

The reaction in the room was very strong. Male militants screamed that the women were serving a conservative state and police apparatus, which tried to degrade and find fault with revolutionaries. And now women, the very wives of political prisoners, were becoming critics, enemies of the revolution!

These women decided that, for them, there was no difference between men unless that difference was materialized in action, in conduct. A leftist militant is different from a feudal lord not when he says so, but when he actually treats women differently. A woman's experience of a revolutionary man, in his intimate behaviour, is a determining criterion and guarantee of the truthfulness of his claim to be a true revolutionary. The private sphere of a political man has not only to be integrated in practice, but has to be considered one of the key determinants of his revolutionary life. When this was said, chaos set in. The session continued for five hours, with interruptions and insults. Dialogue finally became impossible.

Conclusion: The *Umma* and the Challenge of Individualism(s)

Let me return, now, to the initial question: What happens when a woman disobeys her husband, who is the representative and embodiment of sacred authority, and of the Islamic hierarchy? A danger bell rings in the mind, for when one element of the whole structure of polarities is threatened, the entire system is threatened. A woman who rebels against her husband, for instance, is also rebelling against the *umma*, against reason, order and, indeed, God. The rebellion of a woman is linked to individualism, not community (*umma*); passion, not reason; disorder, not order; lawlessness (*fitna*), not law.

The battle between men and women is an aspect of the battle between good and evil, which is a fundamental form of cosmological conceptualization not only in Islam, but in the Jewish and Christian traditions as well. The world is not only the scene of competition, but of polarization between two great competitors. And the polarization implies a hierarchy. One side of the hierarchy – that aligned with God – is destined to win over the devil and his allies.

THE GOOD	THE EVIL
God	Devil (*Iblis, Satan*)
Men, Husband	Women, Wife, Desire (*al-sahwa*)
Reason	Passion (*al-hawa*)
Order	Disorder
Law	Lawlessness (*fitna*)
Obedience, Consensus	Rebellion (*nushuz*), Dissent
Pre-defined Sacred, Eternal Plan	Innovation, Freedom
The Collective Interest (*umma*)	Individualism

Recent studies have supported this dualistic way of thinking in Sunni Islam. On the parallels to the Devil, *Iblis* in Muslim thought, Jalal Sadeq al-'Azim's *Critique of Religious Thought* (Dar al-Talia Beirut, 1980) is a concise analysis of the reason–desire dualism. Fatna Ait Sabbah's *The Woman in the Muslim Unconscious* is probably one of the most recent restatements of that analogy.[7]

Sensual involvement with the gross, material world of earthly pleasures is in the private sphere. It takes place in the domestic realm, in the women's world. In this world, access to knowledge is limited. The private sphere is at the bottom of the pyramidal hierarchy. To be a woman is to be excluded from authority (*al-Sultah*) and knowledge (*'ilm*), both being God's attributes. This is precisely what womanhood is about: to be excluded from the sphere of sacred ritualized and collective knowledge, the sphere in which decisions are made according to the divine code, orders formulated, laws promulgated. And yet the authority and knowledge of the masculine would be inconceivable without the obedience and submission of the feminine, of women.

In principle, one might say that everything in the public sphere is male. The public sphere of prophets, imams and caliphs is monosex and homogeneous. The private sphere of women is duosex and heterogeneous; its heterogeneity comes from the existence of women. The public sphere is characterized by orders and laws; the private sphere is under the control of the representative of the public sphere, the husband. He embodies the interests of the Divine and of the law. In relation to women, the man is not in the posture of 'submission', but in command.

To be a man, then, is to be *both* an obedient submitter, in the public realm, to God and his earthly surrogates, who are all males, *and* a master to whom submission is made, in the private realm, where men master women. This is the pyramidal structure of the hierarchy. And it is in this structure that *nushuz*, innovation or women's rebellion, is a threat. Innovation alters the laws, the sacred order, the privilege and hierarchy – all of which are eternal. The believer can only reinterpret; he cannot create, for creation is the monopoly of God.

Thus, women's rebellion raises the entire complex of questions relating to individualism. Individual freedom, which women's rebellion represents, challenges the entire notion of community as primary. However, it is also because individualism is encroaching from another quarter that it poses such a threat when expressed by women as well. That other quarter is capitalism, which is based upon the profitability of individualistic innovation. Capitalism is seen as ferociously aggressive and fiercely individualistic. Arab countries have also become dumping grounds for the goods of the capitalist world: Western arms, films and consumer goods constitute a virtual invasion. Ironically, innovation – the freedom to doubt – is precisely what makes scientific inquiry and the Western ideology of capitalism so strong and successful! And innovation is what makes women's rebellion so subversive from within.

In the struggle for survival in the Muslim world today, the Muslim community finds itself squeezed between individualistic, innovative Western capitalism on the one hand, and individualistic, rebellious political oppositions from within, among which the most symbolically loaded is that of rebellious women. The common denominator between capitalism and new models of femininity is individualism and self-affirmation. Initiative is power. Women are claiming power – corroding and ultimately destroying the foundations of Muslim hierarchy; whence the violence of the reaction and the rigidity of the response. Femininity as a symbol of surrender has to be resisted violently if women intend to change its meaning into energy, initiative and creative criticism.

Notes

1. Abu Hamid al-Ghazali, *Ihja Ulum al-Din* (Halle, 1917).
2. Fatna A. Sabbah, *The Women in the Muslim Unconscious* (Pergamon Press, 1984).
3. Ibid.
4. See Mernissi, 'L'Amour dans les Pays Musulmans', *Jeune Afrique Plus*, January/February 1984.
5. See Abu al-Firash al-Isfahani, *Kitab al-Aghani* (Book of Songs) (Cairo, 1927).
6. See Mus'ab al-Zubairi, *Nasab Quraysh* (ed. E. Lévi-Provençal, Cairo, 1953) Zubairi died in 850.
7. Sadeq Jalal al-Azm, *Critique of Religious Thought* (Arabic; Dar al-Talia, Beirut, 1980).

Index

Abbasids, triumph of the *Jariya* 83-6
Abbassid period (750-945) 72, 77, 81, 83-4
adolescent girls, pursuit of 43-4
al-Afghani, Sa'id 93
AFTURD group 5
Ai'd (religious festivals) 21
A'isha the Mother of Believers 93, 101
A'isha and Politics 93
Ai'sha (Prophet's third wife) 81, 83, 92-3, 101
Algeria, illiteracy 58; *nushuz* 113; statistics on women's labour 66
'Ali Ibn Abi Talib, Caliph 92-3
American army, reasons for defeat of Arab army 8-9
America's soldiers, literate mothers 9
AMEWS (Association for Middle-East Women's Studies) 105
al-'Amili, Zaynab Fawwaz 103
Amin, Ahmad 85-6
ante-natal care, concept 49-52; educated women and 58-59; National Statistical Bureau and 53-4; survey 49, 58
'Approaches' series of books 6
Arab Charter 42
Arab countries, family planning and 50; maternal mortality 51; record investment in education 58; secrecy in financial matters 49
Arab leaders, solitude after Gulf war 61; and their peoples 8, 37; use of the past 7
Arab male, attitude to working wives 64; defender of inequality 78; schizophrenic contradictions in 37; television and 59
Arab Muslim societies, traditional sexual division of labour 66
Arab nationalist movement 67
Arab political dynamics, *qaid* and *hijab* 56-7
Arab press, crimes of honour 50
Arab society, concept of 'women's work' and Arab men 64
Arab statisticians and economists, women in the labour force 66
Arab world, chief educator is woman 10; educated, qualified elite 58; family planning and education of women 60; modern technology and 9-10; radical revolution in 50; static in sex roles 67
Arabian Nights 14, 69-72, 76

Arabic, words for love 111
Arabic libraries, women and 94, 106
Arafa, Mohammed 95-6
Arib (Jariya) 84
al-Asfahani, Abi al-Faraj 70-1
as-sahabiya (disciples) 82-3
asala (authenticity) 73
al-Asiz, Imraat 56
asra (enemy) 85
audio-visual programmes, benefits of 65
al-'Azim, Jalal Sadeq 118
Aziz, Tariq 9
Azza, Moulay Bou 30
Azzimane, Professor Omar 6
Badr, Liana 2
Badran, Margot 102
Bakr, Caliph Abu 115
balghas (loose trousers) 17
Battle of Ohod (625) 99
bay'a (oath of allegiance) 96
Belarbi, Professor Aicha 6
Berbers 80, 85
Berlin Wall 54
Bhutto, Benizar 79, 87
Bid'a (innovation) 39, 111
Biographies of Famous Women in Early Islam 101
birth control, mass education of women and 59
Bourguiba, President 116-17
Bukhari's Hadith 13, 113
business (tharkalah ' alihum) 11
Central African Republic 66
Chaouni, Leila 11
Cherifa, Professor Alaoui 6
Christianity 14
citizenship, as goal for women 57; notions of *qaid* and *hijab* and 55-8
Coca-Cola adverts 86
Code de Statut Personnel 39
colonial period in Muslim world, capitalist technology 67
colonization, women's labour and 14
Conservative Religious Arab male Leaders, feminism and 13
'Cooking Power and Women's Counterpower' 7
Critique of Religious Thought 118

Al-Dahib 97
Daoud, Zakia 3
democracy, Iraqi deaths and 8; primary issue in Muslim World 110; female elite and 60; knowledge and 10
Derminghen, Emile 25
Djebar, Assia 1
Douglas, Mary 26
Draoui, Dorra Mahfoud 7
Duha al-Islam 85
education and technology skills, strong people and 8
Egypt, abolition of slavery (1898) 78; female illiteracy 58; *nushuz* 113; powerful women in history 102
The Eighth of March (feminist magazine) 116
El Kouch, Sida Zohra 28
El Sadaawi, Nawal 1
En Naifar, Rachida 5
al-Faraj al-Isbahani, Abu 85
Fadl (*jariya*) 84
Farida (*Jariya* 84
farnatchi collecting horse-dung 19
al-Fasi, Allal 42
Fath al-Bari 93
father of wars (al-hurub) 10-11
Fatima (Prophet's daughter) 9, 93
female elite, benefits of 60
female slavery 67
feminism, Western capitals and 13
feminists of first century Islam 113-4
first Umayyads, rejection of polygamy and the veil 83-4
Fouad First University 101
France, abolition of slavery (1848) 78
Freud, Sigmund 27, 37
fundamentalists, attitude of those in power to 95; co-education and the veil 51, 61-2; use of the media 104
Gambia 66
Generalisations of Secluded housewives (*Al-Durr al-manthour fi tabaqat rabbat al khodour*) 103
al-ghaba, Usd 82
Ghadir (*jariya*) 84
Gulf oil-exporting countries, female illiteracy 59
Gulf War 4-5, 8, 61
al-Haq, Zia 79

Hadith repertories 92-3
Hadiths, A'isha and 93
Hamawiya 87
Harbi (historian) 116
harem, care of mothers is intervention 51-2; economic realities and 40
hijab (veil) 49-50, 113; care of mothers and 51-2; collective fantasy of 41;
destructuring of the order of 51; and *qaid* 56
hijra era (622-661 AD) 81-2, 84
houri 14, 71-2
hurra (free woman) 85, 87
Hussein, Saddam 9
Husseyn, Princess Quadriya 103
Ibn 'Abd al-Barr 97-8
Ibn 'Asakir, 100-1, 104
Ibn al-Athir 80, 82, 84, 97
Ibn Batalan 104
Ibn Hajar 93
Ibn Hazm 85
Ibn Hazm al-Andaloussi 98
Ibn Hisham 98-9, 104
Ibn Hajar, Shaikh 96
Ibn Khalikan 71
Ibn Manzur 56, 84-5
Ibn Sa'ad 80, 82, 96
illiteracy, chief battle for Arab women 10, 55, 57; saints and 30
ILO study (1981) 63, 65-6; factors in static sex roles 67-8
individualism, crime against the sacred law 111-2; danger to Islam 109-
10; women's rebellion and questions of 119
inequality, consequences of 35, 40-1
inner light (schaela) 3
Iraq 8, 9; pioneering work on female education 58
Al-Isaba fi Tamyiizi al-Sahaba 96
Islam, authoritarian tradition of 112; criteria for participation in 96;
individualism and 109; is religion of knowledge 112-13; religious law and
38, 79; slavery and prostitution in 104; as a tradition is a political act 89;
vast and wide-ranging civilization 90; women in first decades of 81, 100-
2; women as sexual agents 69
Islamic Democratic Alliance (IDA) 79
Islamic Languages, translations through English into Urdu 105-6
'Islamic memory', product of choice 79
al-Jahiz 85, 87
Jalloun, Taher Ben 8

Jamharat Ansab al-'Arab 98
jami'a (mosque where Friday service is held) 25
Jariya 68, 87, 89; history and legend of 69-74, 84; is *qina* 84
jawari 14, 70-1, 84; Abbasids and 81
Judaism 14
Junejo, Khan 79
'kaadat' (menstruating) 56
Ka'b, Nussaiba Bint 99
Kahhala, Omar 101
al-Khaal, Zaat 88-9
'*al-khubth*' (wickedness combines with meanness) 56
Khaddoura, Zahiya Moustapha 93, 101
Khadija (wife of the Prophet) 81, 99
Khamlichi, Professor Moulay Ahmed 6
Kharijites movement 81
Khawlah Bint Ta'laba 82
Kitab al-Aghini 70
Kitab al-Isti'ab 98-9
Kitab Nassab Goraich 98
Kitab al-Nisa 96-7
Kurds 80, 85
Lalla Nfissa (Algerian female saint) 28
Lamalif 3
as Lisan al-Arab 55, 84
L'Avenir 116-17
law and economic structures, changes in 42-3
Law Faculty (Rabat) 6
Liberia 66
Madagascar 66
Maghreb 23; disintegrating agrarian economies of 30; people of 3, 5, 7; recreation of 5
Mahbouba 84
'*al-makr*' (premeditated desire to destroy) 55-6
male administrative efficiency, female reproduction 49
male saints, as anti-heroes 29-31
Mali 66
Mao's China 38
Marabout (Sanctuary) 21, 41
Al-Masamida (region) 28
al-Massoudi 71
Mas'udi (historian) 80, 84
al-Mawsili, Ibrahim 88

Mecca 4, 23
Medieval history, women's rights and 95-6
Medieval Islam, sex roles in 68-9
medieval religious heritage, women's contribution to Muslim economies 63
Medina, Prophet's days at 87, 95
'medina-telegraph' 46
'medina-theory', new 46-8
Mediterranean man, attitude to women 44; natural forces and 34-5; virgin and 34
The Merchant's Daughter and the Son of the Sultan 16-20
Mimouna, Lalla 30
Ministry of Education 55
Ministry of Health and Planning (Morocco) 47, 55
modern technology, Arab world and 9-10
'modernization' 35
Mohammad V (Tangiers) 42
Moroccan banks, Casablancan bourgeoisie 86
Moroccan Branch of the Arab Writers' Federation 117
Moroccan census (1982) 64-5
Moroccan Family Law (1957) 68
Moroccan males, attitude to working wives 64
Moroccan research collectives 5-6
Moroccan women, contraceptives and 47-8; education and 42; reality of their lives 14; urbanization process and 15, 20
Morocco 11, 13, 52, 113; abolition of slavery (1922) 78; changes in the family 42-3; elections 15; female illiteracy 26, 58-9; ideas about beautiful women 87; radical revolution 50; schooling for men 59; statistics on women's labour 66; survey on contraceptive use 58; very high birth rate 46, virginity a social concept 41
Morocco Demographic and Health Survey (1987), results of 52-4, 60
mosque (*masjid*) 25
mosques, sanctuaries and 25
Most Outstanding Women in Both the Arab and Muslim World 101
The Most Famous Women in the Moslem World (*Shihhirat nisa' fi l'alam al-Islam*) 103
mother of battles (umm al-maa'rik) 10
Mothers of the Believers (title) 82
Mu'awiyah 87-8
Mudawana 39; on polygamy and repudiation (1957) 40
al-Munajid, Salah ed-Din 94
Muruj al-dhahab (Les Prairies d'Or) 80

Muslim countries, ante-natal care programmes 52; women's contribution to production 63

Muslim family, effect of repudiation and polygamy 112; men and women in 40; regulation of relations and roles inside 68, 74-5

Muslim Golden Age 14, 69-71; age of absolutism 87; imaginary and historical 70; female slavery and 67-8; 'Muslim political memory' 78

Muslim heritage, exploration of 61; Universal Declaration of Human Rights and 77

Muslim historians, women in their writings 92-3

Muslim League (ML) 79

'Muslim political memory': A chronicle of the life of the Caliph 80-1

Muslim society, *harem* as domestic space 49-50; sexual desegregation and 41

Muslim tradition, *nisa'ist* intellectuals 99

Muslim women, strategies for enhancing the image 100-2

Muslim World, implications of women's disobedience 109, 119-20

nafaqa (needs) 68-9

Al-Naqd al-thati 42

nass (people) 80

nassab material 98

National Statistical Bureau (Morocco 1989) 53-4

nationalization, women's expectations and 14

Nisa' (1985) 116

nisa (women) 94, 106-7

nisa'ist (feminist) 94-5; intellectuals, Muslim tradition and 99; publishing initiatives 105-6; research 104; researchers 98, 102

nuclear family, in Morocco 43

nushuz (rebellion or subversion) 13, 109, 111-15, 119; implications of 115-7

patriarchal Islam, Arab women and 13-14

patriarchal male, emigration and 43; tragedy of 37

Penal Code, sexual act and 36, 39

People's Republic of North Yemen, female illiteracy 58-9

petit-bourgeois women's movement 67

'political memory', cult of the courtesans 87-9; 'normal' place for women 79-80; what to do with anti-democratic 89-90

'politicos' 4, 6

Population Crisis Committee 59

'Portraits of Women; Change and Resistance' 6

post-natal care, place of birth and 51-2

prayer (*sala*) 25

Princess A'ish (Tangiers 1947) 42

'prodigious leaps forward' (*qafza bassima*) 55
'programmes imposed from on high' 6
prostitution, high unemployment and 44; women who work for a wage 65-6
Provençal, Lery 98
Provincial Western feminists, feminism and 13
qaid (destructive power of women) 13, 56-7, 60
Qaraouiyine University, Fez (Morocco) 102
Qiyan (slaves) 94
Quraish Nobility Council 115
Qur'an 13-14, 17, 20, 56, 67-70, 71-72, 82-3
Qur'an Tafsir (explanations, commentaries) women and 92
Quraysh nobles (disciples of the Prophet) 81
Rabat 3, 8, 117
Rachid, Professor Aberrazzak Moulay 6
al-Rahman, Dr. A'isha 'Abd 102
al-Rashid, Harun 88-9
rasul (emissary) 84
reactionary ulema (learned men of religion), femininist tendencies and 42
recognition of space, social changes and 41-2
religious texts, segregation and 41
Résistance cream 1, 4
Révoltes logiques 116
Risala fi al-kayan (essay on slave women) 84
Saadawi, Nawal el 116
Sabbah, Fatna 109, 118
sabya (capture of women and children) 85
sadaq (dowry) 39
Said, Moulay Abdallah Ou 30
sainthood, male-defined femininity and 27-9
saints, origins of 30
Sakina Bint al-Hussein 83, 86, 102, 113, 114-5
sala (prayer) 25
Salafieh movement 42
Salé 22-3
al-Sanykh, Hannaan 1
sanctury, as Anti-establishment arenas 25-6; prolific literature about 25; provide women with space 31; sexuality and fertility and 27; society's contradictions and 23; as therapy 23-5
Saudi Arabia, slavery in 79
Saudi Princess 50

Sebar, Hassan 42
Second World War 72, 103
seduction of young women, class basis of 43-4
Sehb Edhab (Morocco) 40
sex roles, defined by Qur'an 68, 74-5
sexes, lack of understanding between 35-7
sexual act, schizophrenic transaction 44
Sha'arawi, Huda (1879-1924) 102
shari'a(religious laws) 93, 100; fixed in Medieval period 73; masculinity and femininity and 65
Sharif, Nawaz 79
Sheherezade is not Moroccan (*Chahrazad n'est pas marocaine*) 11
Shi'a movement 80, 93
Shihabi, Sakina 101-2
Sid El Gomri 21-2
Sidi Ben Achir 22
Al-Sira Al-Nabawiya 98-9, 104
sisterhood, class and culture and 16
Siyar a'lam al-nubala 97
social schizophrenia, men and 38-9
soujoùd (the prostration of ritual) 25
South Yemen, female illiteracy 58
al-Suyuti 85
sub-Saharan Africa, statisticians on women's labour 66
Sunni movement 93, 118
Sura 48 verse 25 (The Victory) 82
Sura II, Verse (228) 68
Sura of Yusuf 55-6
al-Tadili, Abu Yaqub 28
Tabari (historian) 80, 82, 84, 97-8, 104
Al-Tabqat al-Kubra 82, 96
Tafsir 82
Tagurrami, Lalla 28-9
Talha, A'isha Bint 83, 86, 113
tarikh (chronicled history) 80-1
Tarikh Dimashq (History of Damascus) 100
Tarikh al-umam wa al-muluk 80, 97
Al-Tasawwuf ila rijal al-tasawwuf 28
Tayyabi, Dr. Aida 101
television, statistics for 54, 55
television, use in family planning strategies 60
television, women in adverts 86

Third World, cost of programmes of maternal care 53; self-congratulatory statistics and 54-5; view of women and 26, 63
Third World politics, saints' rituals and 31
Thousand and One Nights 84
Tiffelent, Imma 28
Tunis writing workshop (May 1991) 5-6
Tunisia, abolition of slavery (1890) 78; education in 59; statistics on women's labour 66
Turks 85
Uçok, Dr. Bahriye 102
Umayyad period 81, 83-4
Umm Salma (wife of the Prophet) 81-2
Umma (nation) 80; challenge of individualism 118-20; fear in (1990s) 112-13
ummahat al-muminin (title for wives of the Prophet) 82
UNICEF 51
United nations, programmes targeted at women 51
Universal Declaration of Human Rights 77
Usd al-ghaba 97
virginity, aim of institution 35; Arab countries and 38; artificial 34-6, 41, 44; social nature of 39
Western feminists, beliefs about Arab women 15-16
Western scholars, 'Moroccan personality structure' 26
Westernization, opposition to 67
'What was Written on the Subject of Women' 94
woman saints, categories of 28; problems of sexuality and reproduction 27-8
women, consciousness regarding gender issues 112; dissemination strategies and 104-5; economic dimension of 64; education and politics 58; effectiveness of programmes targeted at 53-4; fundamentalists and 95; in game of politics in the past 89; historical sources of discipleship 96-100; illiteracy 57-8; link with nature 34-5; low price for their labour 74; marriage 43; phobic attitude of community towards 42; religious histories and 92; and revolutionary men 117; right to Paradise 82; sancturies and 23-4; sexual act responsibility of 36; sexual services rendered by 44-5; share of power and control 27; subordination to men 35; their fertility and the economy 46-7; therapeutic network 25; trickery and 40-1; use of writing by 116
women as disciples, epic years of Islam 81-3
'Women in th Algerian Revolution' 116
Women who Exercised Political Power in History (*Al Nisa' al-hakimat fi al-tarikh*) 102-3

Women's News (*Akhbar al-Nisa*) 93-4
Women's Rights in Islam 95
The Woman in the Muslim Unconscious (1984) 109, 118
writing, authority and 4; benefits of 1-2, 7; true, a quest 6; use by women 116
'written memory' 80
wronged (*madluma*) 24
Yazza, Bou 29
Yemen, slavery and 79
you are repudiated (*'anti Talik*) 86
Zanj (Sudanese blacks) 80
Zaynab Bint Jahch (wife of the Prophet) 81
Zidane, Moulay 28
Zrioual, Professor Fatema 6
Al-Zubeiri, Abi Abdullah ibn Mus'ab 98, 114

Zed Books Ltd gratefully acknowledges the following publishers for permission to reprint from their works:

Chapter 1
'L'ecriture vaut mieux qu'un lifting', *Tunisiennes en devenir*. Tunis: Ceres Productions 1992.

Chapter 2
'Reconstruire Bagdad', Fatima Mernissi, *Charazad n'est pas Marocaine*. Casablanca: Editions le Fennec, 1991.

Chapter 3
'Morocco: The Merchant's Daughter and the Son of the Sultan' by Fatima Mernissi, in *Sisterhood is Global: The International Women's Movement Anthology*, edited by Robin Morgan, Copyright © 1984 by Robin Morgan.

Chapter 4
'Women, Saints and Sanctuaries', *Signs: Journal of Women in Culture and Society*, The University of Chicago Press, Chicago, Illinois, 1997, Vol. 3 No.2.

Chapter 5
'Virginity and Patriarchy', in *Women's Studies International Forum*, reprinted with permission from Pergamon Press Ltd, Oxford OX3 OBW, UK and the author.

Chapter 7
'Women's Work', Halim Barakat, *Contemporary North Africa: Issues of Development*. Georgetown University Center for Contemporary Arab Studies, Washington DC.

Chapter 8
'Le Jariya et le Khalife', *Femmes et Pouvoirs*, Casablanca, Editions le Fennec, 1990.

Chapter 9
'Women in Muslim History', Jay Kleinberg, *Retrieving Women's History*, Berg Publications, Oxford, 1988.

Chapter 10
'Femininity as Subversion,' Diana Eck, *Speaking of Faith: Women, Religion and Social Change*. Philadelphia: New Society Publishers, 1986.